All About My Mother

Pedro Almodóvar is generally regarded as Spain's most important and influential filmmaker. His films include: *Pepi, Luci, Bom* (1980), *Labyrinth of Passion* (1982), *Dark Habits* (1983), *What Have I Done to Deserve This?* (1984), *Matador* (1985–6), *Law of Desire* (1986), *Women on the Verge of a Nervous Breakdown* (1987), *Tie Me Up! Tie Me Down!* (1989), *High Heels* (1991), *Kika* (1993), *The Flower of My Secret* (1996), *Live Flesh* (1997), *All About My Mother* (1999), *Talk to Her* (2002), *Bad Education* (2004) and *Volver* (2006). For *All About My Mother*, Almodóvar won an Oscar for Best Foreign Language Film, in addition to over fifty major international awards, including the Golden Globe, the César, three European Film Awards, two BAFTAs and seven Goyas.

Samuel Adamson's plays include: *Southwark Fair* (National Theatre), *Fish and Company* (National Youth Theatre/Soho Theatre), *Clocks and Whistles* (Bush Theatre), *Grace Note* (Peter Hall Company/Old Vic), *Drink, Dance, Laugh and Lie* (Bush/Channel 4), *The Playhousekeepers* (Private Drama), *Some Kind of Bliss* (NT Platform) and contributions to the 24 *Hour Plays* (Old Vic) and *A Chain Play* (Almeida Theatre). Adaptations include: Ibsen's *Pillars of the Community* (NT) and *A Doll's House* (Southwark Playhouse); Chekhov's *Three Sisters* (Oxford Stage Company/Whitehall Theatre) and *The Cherry Orchard* (OSC/Riverside Studios); Schnitzler's *Professor Bernhardi* (Dumbfounded Theatre/Arcola Theatre/Radio 3); and Bernhard Studlar's *Vienna Dreaming* (NT Studio). Radio includes: *Tomorrow Week* (Radio 3). Film includes *Running for River* (Directional Studios/Krug). He was Pearson Writer in Residence at the Bush in 1997/8.

also by Samuel Adamson

DRINK, DANCE, LAUGH AND LIE
SOUTHWARK FAIR
PILLARS OF THE COMMUNITY
(Ibsen)

published by Amber Lane Press

CLOCKS AND WHISTLES
GRACE NOTE

published by Samuel French Ltd

THREE SISTERS (Chekhov)
THE CHERRY ORCHARD (Chekhov)
A DOLL'S HOUSE (Ibsen)

published by Oberon

PROFESSOR BERNHARDI (Schnitzler)

All About My Mother

based on the film by

PEDRO ALMODÓVAR

a play by

SAMUEL ADAMSON

faber and faber

First published in 2007
by Faber and Faber Limited
3 Queen Square, London WC1N 3AU

Typeset by Country Setting, Kingsdown, Kent CT14 8ES
Printed by CPI Antony Rowe, Eastbourne

A stage adaptation based on the film *Todo sobre mi madre*
(All About My Mother) written and directed by Pedro Almodóvar
and produced by El Deseo SA, Renn Productions and France 2 Cinéma
by arrangement with El Deseo DA, SLU (www.eldeseo.es)

A CIP record for this book
is available from the British Library

ISBN 978-0-571-23952-8

2 4 6 8 10 9 7 5 3 1

Introduction

In Pedro Almodóvar's first full-length film, *Pepi, Luci, Bom and Other Girls on the Heap* (1980), a bearded lady burlesques a Tennessee Williams play. In *Dark Habits* (1983), a Mother Superior snorts heroin in front of a picture of Bette Davis. In *What Have I Done to Deserve This?* (1984), a writer looks to Truman Capote for inspiration. In *Matador* (1985–6), a father seems present by his absence. In *Kika* (1993), a make-up artist waxes lyrical about almond-shaped eyes. And in *The Flower of My Secret* (1996), a nurse called Manuela acts in seminars for the National Transplant Organisation with a raw emotion that leaves her doctor colleagues discomfited and her audience curious as to what she's hiding.

We meet Manuela again – as well as a Williams play, a Davis picture, a Capote enthusiast, an absent father and almond-shaped eyes – in *All About My Mother* (1999), the film for which Almodóvar won the Academy Award for Best Foreign Language Film in 2000. The Oscar recognised his new-found maturity as a filmmaker: when he revisited Manuela, he produced one of his most complex, compassionate characters; when he decided to reveal what she was hiding, why she had access to heartache, he produced his most affecting, cohesive story.

The cohesion was new. *All About My Mother* is about actors and acting, homosexuality, nursing, heart transplants, transvestism, the art of creation, drugs, prostitution, Barcelona, fatherhood, loss of faith, Aids, the end of the *movida* (the underground youth movement that exploded in Madrid and other Spanish cities after

v

the death of Franco), surrogate families, Lorca, plastic surgery, age, love, writing and Hollywood. In lesser hands, it might have been a hotchpotch, but Almodóvar wraps his subjects around the simple story of Manuela's search for her son Esteban's father with such elegance that nothing is extraneous. Every character and theme is intrinsic to the plot; each line and image resonates.

This smoothness distinguished the film from *Pepi, Luci, Bom* and *Labyrinth of Passion* (1982), Almodóvar's gloriously filthy, rough-and-ready accounts of the *movida*; and from his twisted black comedies *Tie Me Up! Tie Me Down!* (1989) and *Kika*. Where, say, a transvestite in *Pepi* has one hysterical stand-alone scene; or where a death in *Kika* is outrageously improbable, in *All About My Mother*, the transvestite (with almond-shaped eyes) is integral to the story, and the death all too real. Where once Almodóvar irreverently parodied a Williams play in a sequence that didn't have much to do with anything, in *All About My Mother* he ingeniously lodged one – *A Streetcar Named Desire* – in the heart of the story.

The death of Esteban was inspired by a similar sequence in John Cassavetes' 1977 film *Opening Night*. On a first viewing, it's a cruel shock: until he dies, we presume Esteban is our protagonist. Played by the charismatic Eloy Azorín and lovingly filmed by Almodóvar, Esteban's tantalisingly close bond with Manuela is conveyed via a series of domestic incidents that recall an enviable relationship between a grandmother and grandson in *What Have I Done to Deserve This?* Mother and son eat together, watch a movie together, wait for someone in the rain together. Nothing prepares us for tragedy: Esteban's teenage obsessions – *Streetcar*, Davis, Capote, his absent father, a famous actress – suggest a gentle tale about coming of age, or perhaps coming out.

Esteban's death forces Manuela into a confrontation with her past: that is, with the *movida* and the pre-Aids, pre-Olympics beach of the Barceloneta, a drug-filled, sexually unconventional world, 'a splendour of *chiringuitos* (seafood kiosks) and freedom'. With this return to the place Esteban was conceived, new characters are introduced and ones met only fleetingly in the opening sequence reappear. But they are all connected to Esteban. His last plea to his mother – 'Some day you will have to tell me all about my father!' – is the engine for *everyone's* story. After Manuela answers the plea, there is a climactic 'miracle' – but one that seems utterly plausible – and a second Esteban replaces the first.

This classical structure is one of the many reasons *All About My Mother* has become a play in English ahead of Almodóvar's other films (1987's brilliantly constructed *Women on the Verge of a Nervous Breakdown*, essentially a filmed farce, is almost too obvious a candidate). But, as per a wish of Almodóvar's, the play is not a replication of the film. It speaks in its own theatrical language. It has plot and story points the film does not, it has new characters, the chronology has been altered, some things have been moved into the light where others have gone to shade.

After I delivered my first draft, I met with Almodóvar in Madrid. He seemed a bit suspicious of anything that was too close to his movie and intrigued by anything I'd written that departed from it. On several occasions he said to me, 'You must draw on what you need to draw on to make it into a play; it must be its own thing!' Which is exactly what *All About My Mother* and all his films are, irrespective of their homages and references.

The *All About My Mother* you're holding is my reimagined *play* of *All About My Mother*: it could take place in any empty space with live actors, but there would be no point filming it. It could be done with a complicated set with flying walls, projections and rain, or it could be done with a few chairs, a box of props and a company that never leaves the stage. The film will exist for ever, its very own thing. This play, and productions of it, can be their very own things as well.

*

Thanks to Kate Pakenham, Beth Byrne and Caro Newling; to Bárbara Peiró, Agustín Almodóvar and everyone at El Deseo; to the original cast and the actors who helped workshop the play, especially Anastasia Hille, Rufus Sewell and Naomi Frederick; to Katie Haines, Richard Porter, David Leveaux, Rachel Wagstaff and Indhu Rubasingham.

Special thanks to Tom Cairns; to Daniel Sparrow for commissioning the play; and to Pedro Almodóvar for his wonderful film, and for graciously giving me so much freedom.

This play is for my parents.

Samuel Adamson,
London, August 2007

All About My Mother was first produced by The Old Vic, Daniel Sparrow, Neal Street Productions, Dede Harris and Debra Black at The Old Vic, London, on 4 September 2007 with the following cast:

Esteban Colin Morgan
Manuela Lesley Manville
Nina Cruz Charlotte Randle
Huma Rojo Diana Rigg
Agrado Mark Gatiss
Sister Rosa Joanne Froggatt
Mother Eleanor Bron
Doctor / Actor / Lola Michael Shaeffer
Alicia / Nurse Yvonne O'Grady
Mario del Toro / Gynaecologist Bradley Freegard
Client / Alex Robert Galas
Nun / Actress Eileen Nicholas
Isabel Lucy-Anne Holmes

Directed by Tom Cairns
Designed by Hildegard Bechtler
Costumes designed by Moritz Junge
Music by Alberto Iglesias
Stage Score by Ben and Max Ringham
Lighting by Bruno Poet
Sound by Christopher Shutt

Characters

Esteban, *seventeen*
Manuela, *his mother, late thirties*
Nina Cruz, *an actress, twenties*
(*plays Stella in* A Streetcar Named Desire)
Huma Rojo, *an actress, a certain age*
(*plays Blanche in* Streetcar)
Agrado, *transvestite, forty*
Sister Rosa, *a nun, twenty-six*
Mother *to Sister Rosa, fifty to sixty*

Doctor
Alicia, *a psychologist*
Mario del Toro, *an actor, twenties*
(*plays Stanley in* Streetcar)
Client
Nun
Alex, *the stage manager*
Gynaecologist, *male*
Nurse
Isabel, *an actress*
(*plays Eunice in* Streetcar)
Actress (*plays Matron in* Streetcar)
Actor (*plays Doctor in* Streetcar)
Lola, *transvestite, forty*

ALL ABOUT MY MOTHER

Dialogue from other plays is indented.
[Dialogue in square brackets is optional.]

Scene numbers are given for rehearsal purposes
but often scenes overlap or the action is continuous:
fluidity is key.

Act One

ONE

A spotlight, a microphone. Esteban, seventeen, steps into the light, takes the microphone, taps.

Esteban One, two, two.

I found this old photo of my mother last night. She looks young. She's standing in front of a shack on some beach, and she's wearing this massive straw hat, and she's smiling like she's tripping; my guess is mescaline. It's like a portal into a time I wasn't alive – but I'm not allowed through, because the photo's been ripped in half. I'm seventeen today, but I look older. I've got the face of a boy who lives alone with his mother. Special, serious . . . a thinker, a writer. I went to her room and found piles of old photos . . . every one has a piece torn away. She has to realise, I don't give a shit what he did to her when they were together, I need to understand who he was.

He puts the microphone down, retreats from the light. It starts to rain.

TWO

Manuela, late thirties, on an ugly plastic chair, grief-stricken. With her, a Doctor in a white coat and a psychologist, Alicia. They are pooled in unforgiving light.

Doctor Unfortunately, señora . . .

Manuela No . . . I just saw him, he was breathing . . .

Doctor The life-support.

Manuela A coma?

Doctor No . . . the machine is pumping oxygen inside his body.

Manuela Then he could pull through. He's strong.

Doctor Brain death is not an easy thing to understand. There's no hope. I'm sorry.

Manuela's grief overtakes her. She wails till it's almost unbearable. The Doctor becomes uncomfortable. Alicia remains calm.

Señora . . . did your son ever . . . talk about death . . . when he was alive?

Manuela He was a boy . . . why would he talk about death?

Doctor Sometimes even young people make decisions about their bodies . . . what should happen in the case of an accident. Señora, your son's organs could be used in a transplant.

Manuela Someone could save him?

Doctor Not quite. Vice versa.

Alicia What my colleague means is that your son could help to save the lives of other patients. But we'd need your consent.

Manuela You want to mutilate him?

Doctor No, it's an internal operation, very simple.

Manuela Who would you give them to?

Doctor The patients who need them most.

Manuela Muslims?
  These filthy rich Arabs who go round buying organs to flog on the black market?

Doctor Señora, Spain is part of the European Pain for Organ –

Alicia (*corrects him, sotto voce*) Plan.

Doctor Part of the European Pan for Organ –

Alicia Plan.

Doctor – *Plan* for Organ Donation.

He's perspiring; he gestures to Alicia in frustration; she indicates he should continue.

The recipient could be any race or creed.

Manuela I'd want them to stay in Madrid.

Doctor You wouldn't have that / choice –

Manuela Prove to me he's dead!

Doctor The National Transplant Organisation has / procedures –

Manuela Let me see him –

Doctor Please, / señora –

Manuela I said let me see him!

Enter Esteban, wet from the rain, in a shaft of light. Manuela clocks him mid-wail.

Doctor Señora?

Manuela I –

She seems on the verge of speaking to Esteban, then resumes her grief.

Doctor Is there someone else we can contact?

Manuela No.

Doctor Then will you sign a consent?

Manuela You're full of shit! I read about the man who came to this hospital for a vasectomy and left without a foreskin.

Doctor What?

How the hell am I supposed to respond to that!?

Alicia OK, let's stop.

The harsh light is flicked off, room lights on: this is a seminar in a hospital lecture room/hall. A cameraman/woman has been filming them, the simulation transmitted in real time on to a monitor/screen for the lecture-room audience. Alicia picks up the microphone.

So, what happened?

Doctor I'm sorry, Alicia . . . it's just . . . that seemed insane . . .

Alicia Perhaps. But some people *are*.

Doctor I mean . . . well . . . I don't think she'd say that.

Alicia Manuela? Manuela?

Manuela She's a grieving mother, we have no idea what she'd say.

Sorry . . . my son.

Everyone turns to look at him.

Esteban Hello.

Alicia Your son?

Manuela (*sotto voce*) What are you doing here . . . ?

Alicia Manuela . . . he should leave. OK, everyone, let's play it back and see what we'd change.

She rewinds with a remote: we now see the simulation the lecture room sees on the monitor/screen. Esteban is fascinated. Manuela approaches him.

Film Doctor . . . the machine is pumping oxygen inside his body.

Film Manuela Then he could pull through. He's strong.

Film Doctor Brain death is not an easy thing to understand. There's no hope. I'm sorry.

Alicia (*pauses replay*) Not bad, so far. (*Fast-forwards film.*)

Manuela Esteban.

Esteban I'm trying to watch, Mama. (*Produces a notebook.*)

Manuela You heard her . . .

Esteban You're amazing. That doctor can't act for shit.

Manuela Shhh! Hospital staff only; you'll get me fired.

Esteban I've got to see this –

By which point Alicia has pressed 'pause', ready to recommence. The room's attention is on them.

Alicia Manuela?

Manuela Go. Go!

She returns to the chair. Esteban is transfixed. Alicia presses 'play'.

Film Manuela I'd want them to stay in Madrid.

Film Doctor You wouldn't have that / choice –

Film Manuela Prove to me he's dead!

Film Doctor The National Transplant Organisation has / procedures –

Film Manuela Let me see him –

Film Doctor Please, / señora –

Film Manuela I said let me see –

Alicia pauses the replay on an image of Manuela.

Alicia Why do you think it broke down?

Doctor I got flustered by her racism.

Alicia Exactly: you judged her. Manuela was clever to act it like that – as if the relative hadn't grasped it yet. (*To lecture hall.*) We try to introduce the subject of donation quickly . . . but it's not possible till the death has been understood . . . We'll do it again.

The Cameraman/woman flicks on the filming light. The simulation – and simultaneous transmission – recommences.

Doctor/Film Doctor We did everything we could.

Manuela/Film Manuela I don't understand you.

Doctor/Film Doctor Señora, unfortunately . . .

Manuela/Film Manuela (*chokes on grief*) My son . . . my son . . . Please, my son . . .

The real Manuela is dwarfed by her cinematic self. Esteban stares at both.

Esteban Mama?

THREE

Esteban opens a door.

Esteban Mama?

He sneaks into a room. A noise, off; he starts. He finds a shoebox high on a shelf or in a drawer, rummages through it. He finds some photographs, leafs through them; stops and stares at one.

Manuela's Voice Esteban?

Esteban pockets the photograph quickly, puts the shoebox back, rushes to another room.

FOUR

Out of the darkness, lighted candles on a birthday cake, held by Manuela. Esteban quickly grabs a book, settles, pretends to read.

Manuela's Voice Esteban? Esteban?
Why didn't you answer?

Esteban I did.

Manuela Happy birthday.

Esteban It's not my birthday.

Manuela It's just gone midnight. Come on, quickly.

Esteban (*blows candles out*) Shall I tell you what I wished for?

Manuela Of course not. (*Cuts cake.*) What are you reading?

Esteban Mama . . .
What do you think about when you cry in those transplant simulations?

Manuela Nothing. I don't cry.

Esteban You did.

Manuela And you shouldn't have barged in . . .

Esteban But where did you learn to act like that?

Manuela Nowhere. I just do it.

Esteban You must think about something.

Manuela No. I just empty my mind.

Esteban My father?

Manuela What makes you say that?

Esteban It was so real.

Manuela Eat. Go on, you need to put on some weight. What if you have to support me? You'll never make it on the streets, thin like that.

Esteban Rent boys don't need body fat . . . they need big dicks.

Manuela (*shocked*) Wash your mouth.

Esteban You started it.

Manuela I was joking.

Esteban What about you?

Manuela What about me?

Esteban Would you go on the game for me?

Manuela I've done everything in the world for you, Esteban. Everything.
I did get you more than cake, you know.

Esteban I don't need presents.

Manuela Really?

Esteban If I had to ask you for one thing, Mama, it wouldn't be some T-shirt or CD.

Manuela Right.

Esteban I'm an adult.

Manuela Then I'll just have to return these . . . (*Fans herself with tickets.*) tickets . . . to a certain play . . . starring a certain famous actress.

Esteban Huma Rojo?

Manuela Huma who?

Esteban But it's her last night in Madrid tomorrow!

Manuela Perhaps I queued for hours.

Esteban can't contain his excitement. Manuela withdraws playfully; he tackles her.

Esteban No!

Manuela Uh-uh-uh . . .

Esteban Mama . . . Huma / Rojo!

Manuela If you've gone off her in your old age . . .

Esteban How did you know?

Manuela Why wouldn't I?

Esteban kisses her. She notices his notebook, and as if in exchange for the tickets, picks it up. He takes it back.

Esteban Don't panic, there's nothing in here about you.

Manuela Glad to hear it.

But Esteban's smile suggests otherwise. Manuela makes to leave. Out of the darkness, lighted candles on a birthday cake, held by Nina Cruz, twenties.

Esteban You *do* think about my father, don't you?

Manuela I'm a nurse, Esteban, not an actress.

Nina Blanche. Blanche.

Esteban If you acted, I'd write great roles for you.

They stare at each other.

Manuela Brush your teeth.

FIVE

Esteban and Manuela, sitting side by side, watching Nina: she is Stella in Tennessee Williams' A Streetcar Named Desire. *She is pregnant. Huma Rojo, a certain age, is Blanche DuBois. Mario del Toro, twenties, is Stanley.*

11

Nina *as* **Stella** Blanche?

Huma *as* **Blanche** Oh, those pretty, pretty little candles! You ought to save them for baby's birthdays. Oh, I hope candles are going to glow in his life and I hope that his eyes are going to be like candles, like two blue candles lighted in a white cake!

Mario *as* **Stanley** What poetry!

Blanche His auntie knows candles aren't safe, that candles burn out in little boys' and girls' eyes, or wind blows them out and after that happens, electric light bulbs go on and you see too plainly . . .

Stanley Sister Blanche, I've got a little birthday remembrance for you.

Blanche Oh, have you, Stanley? I wasn't expecting any, I – I don't know why Stella wants to observe my birthday! When you – reach twenty-seven! Well – age is a subject that you'd prefer to – ignore!

He is holding a little envelope towards her.

Blanche What is it? Why, why – Why, it's a –

Stanley Ticket! On the Greyhound! Tuesday!

Stella rises abruptly and turns her back. Blanche clutches her throat and runs into the bathroom. Coughing, gagging sounds are heard.

Stella You didn't need to do that. You needn't have been so cruel.

Stanley Delicate piece she is.

Stella She is. She was. You didn't know Blanche as a girl. Nobody was tender and trusting as she was. But people like you abused her, and forced her to change.

She catches hold of his shirt.

Why did you do this to her?

Stanley I done nothing to no one. Let go of my shirt. You've torn it.

Stella I want to know why.

Stanley When we first met, you thought I was common . . . and how you loved it . . .! Wasn't we happy together? Wasn't it all OK? Till she showed here?

Stella feels the child inside her palpitate, grabs her stomach, finds furniture to lean on.

Hoity-toity, describing me as an ape. Hey, what is it, Stell?

Stella Take me to the hospital.

He supports her with his arm and goes outside. Blanche comes out.

Blanche
Say it's only a paper moon,
Sailing over a cardboard sea.
But it wouldn't be make-believe
If you believed . . .

She blows the candles out. Whoosh.

SIX

An enormous image of Huma's face, part of the front-of-house of a theatre:

HUMA ROJO
as Blanche DuBois in
A STREETCAR NAMED DESIRE
by Tennessee Williams
also starring
NINA CRUZ *and* MARIO DEL TORO

13

It is raining. Manuela and Esteban are huddled under an umbrella on the other side of the street. Manuela is wearing a raincoat and clutching a theatre programme. Esteban is clutching his notebook.

Esteban We're not leaving.

Manuela Yes, we are.

Esteban I have to get her autograph.

Manuela It's pouring, we'll catch our deaths . . .

Thunder.

Esteban, really . . .

Esteban She's incredible, Mama, I'll never get a chance like this again.

He makes for the theatre; traffic, headlights.

Manuela All right, all right . . . For goodness' sake, get under the umbrella.

They wait.

Esteban Did Stanley rape Blanche?

Manuela Yes. She didn't lose her mind, he took it from her.
What if no one comes out?

An actress (Isabel) comes out of the stage door, rushes off. Thunder, heavier rain.

Esteban I don't think I'll ever see another performance like that. The definitive Blanche.

Manuela She was good.

Esteban You preferred Nina Cruz, didn't you?

Manuela Actually, I could take or leave Nina Cruz.

Esteban But I saw you crying.

Manuela It was the writing, not the acting.
I've been in *Streetcar*.

Esteban Really?

Manuela When I was young, I belonged to an amateur company.

Esteban I knew it!

Manuela I played Stella. I was pretty good.
Your father was Stanley.

Esteban stares at her.

She could be ages. This is crazy.

Esteban (*takes photograph from his pocket*) Where was this photo taken?

Manuela Where did you get that?

Esteban Look at you . . . you look so young. But modern, too. Are you stoned or something? Drugs down by the sea?!

Manuela Where, Esteban?

Esteban A shoebox. There were hundreds of them.

Manuela You shouldn't be looking through my things.

Esteban How else would I know anything about what you were like before I was born? Why is half missing?

Mario comes out of the stage door, rushes off.

You just ripped my father away, as if he never existed?

Manuela It's complicated.

Esteban It's not fair! Stop saying, 'He's dead' . . . You have to tell me about him. Who was he? Who? Did he even know about me?

Manuela I'll talk to you when we get home.

Esteban No, Mama –

Manuela I'll tell you everything then.

Esteban You never do! I'm seventeen! Don't you get it? It's like I only have half a life . . . if you're ashamed of him, you must be ashamed of me.

Manuela I promise . . .

But Esteban has winded her. He begins the story for her:

Esteban Eighteen years ago, you left Argentina and came to Madrid . . .

Manuela (*shakes head*) Not Madrid. Barcelona. I left home to be with a friend in Barcelona. But I only stayed a year. Then we ran away.

Esteban You and your friend?

Manuela You and I, Esteban. We got on a train and came to Madrid together. You were inside me.

Esteban Why did we leave?

Huma and Nina come out of the stage door. Huma is wearing a magnificent cape. Headlights capture them, illuminating Huma in the manner of an iconic photograph: the actress, standing against her own theatrically magnified image. Esteban is thunderstruck.

Huma. (*Shouts.*) Señora Rojo?!

Huma looks across to Esteban. He half-waves his notebook at her. Nina walks off into the night. Huma is drawn away by Nina. Noisy traffic, headlights.

Wait, Señora Rojo!

Huma turns towards him and again she is illuminated. She and the boy share a moment, she smiles, the stuff of his dreams. Then it's over, and Huma disappears into the traffic.

Manuela Forget it, Esteban. Come on, let's go home . . .

Esteban Señora Rojo!

Manuela They've gone, it doesn't matter . . . Esteban. Esteban?

Esteban runs into the street suddenly.

Esteban!

Bright headlights pierce the rain. A shocking thump. Manuela drops the umbrella. The wind lifts it and it rolls across the street. Manuela runs towards her son. The rain stops.

Esteban Mama.

Manuela Yes.

Esteban Mama.

The actor playing Esteban removes himself from All About My Mother. *Disconnected sounds creep in: an ambulance, the bleep-bleep of a life support.*

Manuela My son?

The headlights intensify.

SEVEN

Alicia and the Doctor with Manuela, who is on the ugly plastic chair. A familiar image, except Manuela's hair is wet, she is wearing the wet, stained raincoat and she is clutching Esteban's rain- and blood-stained notebook.

Doctor Manuela, we did everything we could.

Bleep.

Unfortunately . . .

Manuela (*chokes on her grief*) My son . . .

Sleep.

Alicia You know what I have to ask you . . . Will you sign the consent?

She puts a pen in Manuela's hand, guides her to sign a release form. Manuela signs, lifelessly. Alicia hands the form to the Doctor, who leaves with it.

I'm so sorry, Manuela . . .

Manuela No . . . no . . . Let me . . .

She tries to stand, her body gives way; Alicia catches her; they are on the ground.

My son . . . my son . . . Please . . .

Bleeeeeeep.

EIGHT

The spotlight, the microphone. Agrado, forty, steps into the light. She is wearing a two-piece Chanel suit. She taps the microphone, peers out nervously.

Agrado One, two, two. Two.

Ladies and gentlemen, could I have your attention please. Good evening. I'm very sorry . . . but something's gone wrong. I could say it's a technical hitch, but that would be a lie: it's human, like most hitches. Suffice to say that owing to circumstances beyond the management's control, we have to cancel. (*To lighting box.*) House lights, please.

House lights up.

There's an usher. See if you can prise a refund out of him.

Then again, if you're open to pleasure, how vile to go back out there, when here you are – in the theatre! (*To someone in front row.*) Oh, hello! Remember me? Under the bridge? I never forget a face. Especially one I first saw from waist height. And your wife, is it? Evening, señora. How quaint, a beard. So retro it's practically chic.

Where was I? Oh yes – I say stay, and I promise to entertain you with the story of my life. Don't leave, it's hell out there; Barcelona is a dump these days, don't you think? (*To lighting box*.) Pablo? Pablo, house lights down, love, they're doing these people no favours . . .

House lights out.

Barcelona? – I spit on Barcelona: nothing but a haven for drag queens. On the streets, you have the whores, the transvestite whores, and nowadays, the drags, and they're killing the whores and trannies; the red light district is like a drag-queen tea party at three a.m. on a Friday. Listen up, drag queens – I see you – transvestism is not a circus! A woman is her hair, her nails, good pouty lips to bitch with. Now . . . with me, you get authenticity. My name is Agrado. It means 'pleasure'. (As we know, one or two of you here tonight have already had the pleasure.) Take a good look at my body. I am my very own project. Tits, two of them, bought in Paris –

[**Voice From Theatre Box** (**Mario**) How much they cost you, love?!

Agrado Premature interjection, honey, I was getting to that.] Seventy thousand pesetas per tit.

Spot flickers.

Impressive, Pablo, I know.
  Eyes, shaped like diamonds –

Spot flickers and dies, utter darkness.

Pablo? Pablo?
  Hello, I'm still here. I'm just telling them all about the / implants –

A roar, a struggle, a barrage of bad language.

A Voice (Client) You filthy tart, come back here!

Agrado's Voice Fucking son of a fuck bitch!

Client's Voice Finish me off!

Agrado's Voice You've got a hand, finish your fucking self off!

Client's Voice Turn / over.

Agrado's Voice Fuck you!

Client's Voice Keep still, bitch!

Agrado's Voice You crab-ridden crackhead troll, get the fuck off me!

A scream.

NINE

Agrado, in a struggle with a Client. She is dressed for the game – i.e., no sign of the Chanel.

Client Stop moving –

Agrado Get out of my house, stalker.

Client We had an agreement –

Agrado You paid for a blow job – you get a blow job.

Client Not enough –

Agrado You want more, find a rent boy, you shirt-lifting cocksucker . . .

Client head-butts Agrado; it gets violent, things smash. Manuela bangs on the door, yells 'Agrado!' and enters. She is soberly dressed, holding a bag of food.

Client You owe me –

Agrado Fucking maniac!

Client laughs menacingly. Manuela grabs a bottle from the bag, thrashes it over Client's head. He groans and goes down. Shock, silence.

Checkmate, motherfucker.
  Who the fuck are you?

Manuela Are you all right?

Agrado Oh my God, what if you've murdered him? Please tell me he's alive . . .

Manuela I heard you / screaming –

Agrado Help, woman, I have to get him out of here! Get up!

They lift Client to his feet. He groans.

This is the last time I service you, you schizophrenic faggot. Oh, stop blubbering. It's a scratch. (*To Manuela.*) Did you really need to bottle him? (*To Client.*) Go and find Ursula under the bridge, she'll put a plaster where it hurts. And don't try it on with any of my neighbours, this is a respectable building.

Client staggers out.

Manuela Agrado.

Agrado Manolita?

Manuela Hello.

Agrado My Manolita? No . . .

Client lurches back in with a roar. Agrado and Manuela scream, but work as a team to punch and push him out.

Shit, what a town! Every demon in hell wants lips on the end of his prick.

She looks at Manuela tearfully; they laugh, they hug, long and hard.

21

Where have you come from?

Manuela I had no idea if you still lived in Barcelona . . .

Agrado Let me look at you . . .

Manuela I've missed you, Agrado.

Agrado Like an angel.
Oh Manolita, Manolita . . .

They hug again.

Eighteen years . . .

Manuela Let's fix you up.

Agrado Not a single word . . .

Manuela finds a cloth, etc.

No fucking letters . . .

Manuela Keep still . . .

She dabs Agrado's face. Agrado seethes from the sting.

Agrado I thought you were dead in a ditch . . . ouch . . .
ouch . . .

Manuela I think you'll live.

Agrado Not one phone call. You forgot me.

Manuela No, Agrado. I thought about you every day.

Agrado I did, too, and I'm not just saying that: see, see –
(*Finds a framed photo.*) I look at the three of us on this
damn beach every day.

Manuela takes the photo, looks at it. Grief threatens.

What?

Manuela Nothing.
I'm tired, that's all . . .

Agrado Manolita. You're back, you're back. You haven't changed.

Manuela Nor have you.

Agrado That's a back-handed compliment; I'm more woman now than I was then, let's face it. (*Re. photo.*) Look at your eyes (thank you, Mexican drugs). That was our time, wasn't it, there on the Barceloneta?

Manuela Yes.

Agrado Things were so different. The whole world was ours. We were free.
And talking of manly shoulders, doesn't Lola think she's the dog's bollocks? The Pioneer! Gorgeous shit, it'd be quite a nice picture if she wasn't in it.

Manuela (*busies herself*) I've brought food, I remember what you like . . .

Agrado But where have you been, Manolita? Why did you disappear? Did you go back to Argentina?

Manuela Madrid.

Agrado What have you been doing?

Manuela Nursing.

Agrado Nursing? Eighteen years? Nothing else?

Manuela Please . . . don't ask me any questions . . .

Agrado But what are you doing here? When did you arrive? Are you going to stay?

Manuela For a while . . . I've found a flat.

Agrado You have a job?

Manuela No . . . I'll need one . . .
Agrado. I'm looking for Lola.

Agrado Ha! ('*Spits*'.)

Manuela She's not here?

Agrado She was, right here. Freeloader, stayed for months . . . I was happy to have her, in spite of it all I love her. Poor thing's been sick as a dog. Same old story, pumping that shit inside, she hasn't got a vein left.

Manuela Where is she now?

Agrado Wherever she disappeared to after she cleared off with half my stuff! Jewellery, money . . . even all my old seventies magazines – my inspiration!

Manuela She hasn't changed . . .

Agrado I've stood by her: we had our tits put on together. That's a sacred bond! Twenty years down the pan. She's too much. Too pretty, fucked-up, lovable, too everything.

Manuela You've no idea where she went?

Agrado I hope she's rotting in the nether regions. Why?

Manuela I have to find her.

Agrado What for?

Manuela Not now . . .

A moment. Agrado sees that she shouldn't press it.

Agrado All right . . . fine . . . (*Cries.*) But don't you pull another disappearing act on me. I like to say goodbye to the people I love, even if it's only so I can bawl my eyes out . . .

Manuela Eat.

Agrado Oh, woman, how do you do it? I'm ravenous . . . Mmn . . . twenty years' worth of hunger, I haven't had a proper meal since 1981. (*Chews, pain.*) Ow. Ouch. If I can't even chew, how am I going to suck?

Manuela I think you're going to have to take some time off work, Agrado.

Agrado Impossible: Lola cleaned me out. (*Picks up a hand mirror.*)

Manuela Perhaps it's time for a career change.

Agrado (*screams*) The Elephant Woman! There isn't a pervert in Barcelona who'd pay!

Manuela Stop feeling sorry for yourself.

Agrado barks. Manuela barks back. They peck each other on the lips, bark again, collapse with laughter – an old friends' ritual – tears threaten, they hug. Suddenly:

Agrado Huh! Manuela! You need work, I need change: we'll go to the nuns.

Manuela Nuns?

Agrado There's someone I want you to meet. Yes. Stick with me. Perfect.
    Don't move.

She disappears. On her own, Manuela picks up the photo again, contains her grief. Agrado returns with a tarty-looking dress.

Try this for size.

Manuela You're not serious?

Agrado These are special sisters who only help women from the streets.

Manuela So?

Agrado So you need slappification, or you'll never get through the door.

Manuela Agrado, I don't need to dress / like a –

Agrado If it doesn't fit we'll have to go out in the morning and buy one, so hurry up.
    Trust me, Manuela. I know what I'm doing.

TEN

A Nun, wearing a simple headscarf, but otherwise in
civilian clothing. Agrado, dressed as she would normally
dress. Manuela, wearing the tarty dress.

Nun Wait here, I'll find her for you.

Agrado Thank you, sister.

Manuela This isn't quite what I was expecting . . .

Agrado They've devoted their lives to rehabilitating
clapped-out tranny whores.

Manuela Is that us?

Agrado Of course not, we're down, but not that down.
Still, you never know, they might have the perfect job.

Manuela How did you find them?

Agrado I met Sister Rosa on the streets. Your filthy mind:
she gives out condoms and needles. So dangerous . . . it's
an apocalypse of plastic tits on my patch, but it's water
off a duck's back to her. Everyone falls in love with Rosa.
    Manolita, you look just like a hooker. I feel so proud.

Enter Sister Rosa, twenty-six.

Sister Rosa Hello, Agrado!

Agrado Good morning, sister.

Sister Rosa Oh, dear: your face!

Agrado I took a little hammering.

Sister Rosa You poor thing!

Agrado All in a night's work. Anyway, this is what I want
to talk to you about. You don't mind?

Sister Rosa No, it's so lovely to see you.

Agrado We want out of the game. Isn't that right, Manolita? We've had it with the streets. This is my oldest friend – and colleague – Manuela.

Manuela Hello.

Sister Rosa Hello. Rosa.

Agrado So we need some new kind of work. Cleaning. Whatever.

Sister Rosa I see . . .

Agrado We want to eat, so it's got to pay.

Sister Rosa Agrado, you know we don't have paid jobs at the refuge! I could find you volunteer work . . . it would depend on your skills. (*Artless.*) What can you do, Manuela, besides sell your body?

Manuela I've . . . worked as a cook.

Sister Rosa Oh . . . we don't need cooks. We have a new programme for picking up litter!

Agrado You mean we'd be volunteer dustbinwomen?

Sister Rosa Or you could come here and make handicrafts. Cross-stitching, dried-flower arranging . . . that would keep you off the streets.

Agrado Tell me about the rubbish collecting?

Sister Rosa I'm sorry, Agrado!

Agrado Never mind, worth a try. Onwards, Manolita. Manuela's Argentinean. Countrywoman of Lola's.

A well-placed sally: neither Sister Rosa nor Manuela expected it.

Manuela You know Lola?

Sister Rosa Yes.

Agrado (*by-the-by, aware of her hand grenade*) Bitch ransacked my flat.

Manuela How?

Sister Rosa She came to us for help a few months ago. She was a bit of a mess. She went cold turkey, I looked after her. One night she just vanished.

Agrado Full of charming habits.

Manuela You haven't heard from her since?

Sister Rosa (*shakes head*) Have you seen her?

Manuela Not for years.

Agrado The lives we led, sister; Barcelona after Franco, you wouldn't believe it.

Manuela and Sister Rosa regard each other.

Sister Rosa I'd really like to say goodbye to her . . . before I go to El Salvador.

Agrado Before you go where?

Sister Rosa El Salvador.

Agrado Really?

Sister Rosa In a couple of weeks.

Agrado Well, sister, I should hitch a ride. I always thought the Third World had my name written all over it.

Sister Rosa Yes, yes, yes! Then I wouldn't be on my own!

Manuela You're going by yourself?

Agrado I *will* find a part of this planet not colonised by drag queens.

Sister Rosa That's probably El Salvador – though they do have insurgents.

Agrado Do they?

Sister Rosa I'm going to replace some nuns who were murdered.

Agrado Perhaps South America isn't really my bag.

Enter the Nun.

Nun Rosa. Your workshop.

Sister Rosa Oh. Can they do it without me?

Nun No.

Sister Rosa Manuela . . . I'd like to talk to you. Can you stay? I'll only be half an hour.

Manuela All right . . . I'll wait.

Agrado Don't mind me.

Sister Rosa Agrado! Cast off like an old sock!

She kisses Agrado twice, rushes out after the Nun.

Manuela Thank you, Agrado.

Agrado It's a start, Manolita. Press her some more; you never know. And when you find Lola, tell her I'll have back the Holy Virgin she stole from my lavatory. What would she want with that – she doesn't believe in anything. Unless she's using it for satanic rituals.
My work is done. La Agrado has left the nunnery.

ELEVEN

A painting – Picasso, ideally, or Chagall. Manuela, Sister Rosa and Sister Rosa's Mother, fifty to sixty. Mother is wearing a paint-splattered smock.

Sister Rosa Picasso.

Manuela Yes. I see that.

Sister Rosa A forgery.

Manuela Oh.

Sister Rosa Mama's a forger!

Mother Rosa. That's incorrect.

Manuela It's . . . incredible.

Sister Rosa I hope you weren't busy, Mama?

Mother You're always welcome, Rosa, you know that. It's just that you never come. At least not by yourself.

Sister Rosa Mama . . . Manuela is a wonderful cook!

Mother has no idea how to respond.

She worked as a chef. In a restaurant!

Mother Remarkable. Such versatility. Did it clash with your . . . other occupation?

Manuela is very ill at ease in Agrado's dress.

Sister Rosa How's Papa?

Mother Fine. He's out walking.

Sister Rosa On his own?

Mother No, with his carer. You've never been to meet her, have you? Would you like tea . . . um . . . Manuela?

Manuela No thank you, señora.

Sister Rosa Mama, I've had the most brilliant idea. Manuela cooks, and since Florinda left you like that / you've been –

Mother Florinda? What do you mean?
(*Looks at Manuela, then back at Sister Rosa.*) Not –?
(*A short laugh.*) My God, Rosa? You're not serious?
(*To Manuela.*) I'm sorry, I had no idea she'd brought you here for this.

Sister Rosa But you don't have the time to cook for Papa / and –

Mother Stop it, Rosa. You think like a child. (*To Manuela.*) Excuse me.

Sister Rosa I so wanted to see Papa . . .

Mother You can. Whenever you like. We miss you.

She looks at her daughter meaningfully, leaves.

Manuela I have to go.

Sister Rosa I'm sorry. Don't worry, it's not over yet.

Manuela Yes it is, Rosa. There's no job for me here . . .

Sister Rosa Stay, please. Please. (*Laughs, oddly desperate.*) She can afford you . . . look at this place! She sells them to all sorts of people, she makes a killing!

Manuela I wasn't expecting you to bring me to your mother's, Rosa. (*Re. dress.*) Look at me. It was sweet of you to do this, but . . . I can find a job on my own.

Sister Rosa You're perfect for her. Don't read anything into it, it's just the way she is.

Manuela The truth is, I was a nurse once so / I can always –

Sister Rosa A nurse – ?

Manuela Rosa: do you know where Lola is?

Sister Rosa No.

Manuela Then I have to go.

Sister Rosa Don't leave me, don't go – please, I mean it.

She suddenly goes pale, closes her eyes, puts her hand to her brow.

Manuela Rosa?

Sister Rosa I –

Manuela Are you all right?

Sister Rosa I'm –

*Rushes out through a different door from the one her
mother used, knocking something over on the way.*

Manuela Rosa –?

*Manuela doesn't know what to do. She picks up the
disturbed item but doesn't get it back in place before
Mother returns: she is compromised even further.*

Mother Rosa –? Oh. Still here. What's she up to now?

Manuela I'm sorry . . .

Mother Yes, so am I. Sorry my gullible daughter is so
sentimental. Thinks she can change the world.
 You know where the door is, slut.

Enter Sister Rosa.

Manuela Goodbye, señora.

Sister Rosa Manuela? No, Mama . . . just a few days . . .
She's also a nurse.

Mother So many strings to her bow.

Sister Rosa She could give Papa his pills . . .

*But it is Mother's house. Sister Rosa holds her hand
out helplessly as Manuela heads for the street,
humiliated.*

It's impossible to help you, Mama, because you're
impossible!

Mother You think I need the help of a whore?

Sister Rosa When you're rude like that I feel ill. And
she's not a whore any more.

Mother How do you know what she is? How long have
you known her?

Sister Rosa Since ten o'clock.

Mother Oh, Rosa, honestly. How did you turn out like
this?

Sister Rosa My work is to help people, even if I've only just met them.

Mother And mine isn't –

Sister Rosa You call this *work*?!

Mother I don't like strangers watching me . . . (*Gestures to painting.*)

Sister Rosa Because you're ashamed! You're a fake! You've squandered your talent on these knock-offs and you're ashamed!

She's gone too far. Both are chastened.

Mother We'll go and find your father. Or stay, wait for him.

Sister Rosa Not today. Next time. (*Apology for outburst.*) I'm sorry.

Mother You're so thin. Are you eating?

Sister Rosa Mama . . .

Mother Rosa, they're not forgeries – they're imitations.

Sister Rosa Deep down . . . you're not like this.

Mother Wait. Please.
This El Salvador thing. Don't go.

Sister Rosa Don't make it harder for me, I'm confused enough as it is.

Mother Of course you are – it'd be simpler to save yourself the bother and put a bullet in your head now.

Sister Rosa I have to go.

Mother That's right, some tart, some Salvadoran gangster: they all mean more to you than your own mother and father.

Sister Rosa Goodbye, Mama.

Mother Take more care. Don't mix yourself up with these people.

TWELVE

Manuela, on the street, mortified by her ordeal. Off, Sister Rosa's plaintive cry:

Sister Rosa's Voice Manuela?

Manuela can't face her. Traffic, and she thinks she sees Esteban:

Manuela Esteban.

Sister Rosa's Voice Manuela!

Manuela Esteban? Esteban!

Car horn; she puts her hands to her face. Then silence. She sits on a bench in a dusty square, tries to pull herself together. Esteban sits next to her.

Why didn't you answer?

Esteban I did. (*Takes a battered book from his pocket.*) Read this to me.

Manuela You know how to read, Esteban.

Esteban Like you used to.

Manuela (*relents, takes book*) Truman Capote. There's a surprise.

Esteban Go on.

Manuela 'I started writing when I was eight – out of the blue –'

Esteban There: others like me!

Manuela 'I didn't know that I had chained myself for life to a noble but merciless master. When God hands you a

34

gift, he also hands you a whip; and the whip is intended solely for self-flagellation.'

Esteban (*takes back book*) Isn't it wonderful?

A moment. Manuela takes Esteban's blood- and rain-stained notebook from her handbag, glances at a page. Enter Nina (as Stella, though inexplicably she isn't wearing a false pregnancy stomach).

Nina Why did you do this to her?

Esteban After you gave me the tickets to *A Streetcar Named Desire*, I had this image of you walking through the corridors of a theatre . . .

Nina Why?

Esteban The image turned into an idea for a story, and I wrote it down.

Enter Mario, as Stanley. Manuela turns a page.

Mario I done nothing to no one.

Esteban 'All About My Mother.'

The notebook is too much for Manuela. She closes it with a grief-stricken thud . . .

THIRTEEN

And she is watching A Streetcar Named Desire. *The seat next to her is empty.*

Stanley Let go of my shirt. You've torn it.

Stella I want to know why.

Stanley When we first met, you thought I was common . . . and how you loved it . . .! Wasn't we happy together? Wasn't it all OK? Till she showed here?

Stella feels the child inside her, though there isn't much to feel, with no false stomach.

Hoity-toity, describing me as an ape. Hey, what is it, Stell?

Stella Take me to the hospital.

He supports her with his arm, etc. Blanche comes out.

Blanche
Say it's only a paper moon,
Sailing over a cardboard sea.
But it wouldn't be make-believe
If you believed . . .

She blows the candles out. Applause.

FOURTEEN

Huma, Nina and actors on the onstage side of the curtain: the entire Streetcar *company has just given its curtain call. Rigging, ropes, fire exits – the real theatre, and the real* All About My Mother *theatre crew. The line of actors doesn't break as it might because everyone's indignant, silent attention is on Nina.*

Huma Nina.

Nina What, Huma?

Huma How could you?

Nina What?

Huma That was a terrible thing to do.

Nina So you think.

Huma Your character is heavily pregnant in Scene Seven. When you do something as stupid as not wear the padding . . . you're vandalising the play and insulting the entire company.

Nina rushes to the dressing room, tearing off her costume.

Nina!

I'm sorry, everybody.

The line of Streetcar *actors breaks, disperses. Alex, the stage manager:*

Alex I don't know what to say . . .

Huma It won't happen again, Alex.

She heads off after Nina as Streetcar *begins to dematerialise: crew clear furniture, sweep, collect props. Perhaps walls and scrims are flown out silently.*

Nina?

She opens a door, steps into her dressing room. It has a door to its own bathroom, the interior of which might be seen by the audience. There are photographs spanning Huma's career and many faces and a poster of Bette Davis enveloped by cigarette smoke. The room/bathroom are marooned in the stage/backstage area, which can still be seen. With the stripping of the Streetcar *set, actors and crew melt away.*

Nina?

Nina (*from bathroom*) I'm here, Huma, don't panic.

Huma closes the door and blocks out the backstage noise. She sits at the mirror, stares. She pulls off her Blanche DuBois wig, and she is all too human.

Huma I'm sorry I had to do that in front of the whole company. I love you, Nina, but that was too much.

Nina It's like living in a fucking nunnery!

Huma No . . . you're punishing me. (*Continues de-Blanching.*)

You also rotated anti-clockwise around the table in Scene One, not clockwise.

Nina comes out of the bathroom, in bra and knickers, screaming hysterically:

Nina What difference does it fucking make which fucking way we turn around the fucking table!

Too much. She pulls her dress on, lights a cigarette.

Huma You can't continue like this.

Nina I'm sorry.

Huma You'll be thrown out of the company . . .

Nina I hate Barcelona, that's all. I'm sick of touring. Sorry . . .

Huma forgives her, kisses her, disappears to bathroom. Nina stares in the mirror. As she does this, enter Manuela through a fire exit door in the back wall backstage. She is no longer wearing Agrado's dress and her hair is tied back soberly. The theatre is now devoid of Streetcar. Dirty, unglamorous, eerily lit by the lacklustre fire exit sign and working lights. Manuela traverses the strange new landscape.

Huma They were still enthusiastic! Catalan audiences are the best!

During the following one-sided conversation, Nina becomes increasingly desperate. She searches her handbag, finds an old drug bag, rubs it against her gums to no effect. She sees Huma's handbag, rifles through it.

I thought we'd go out to dinner? Nina?

Nina Yeah, great.

Huma I've booked.

Nina Good.

Huma Are you hungry? Nina?

Nina I'm still here, Huma, I'm not deaf.
Yeah, starving. Dinner would be lovely. (*At which point she discovers a wadge of cash in Huma's handbag.*) Fucking lovely.

Manuela reaches the dressing-room door. She knocks. Nina starts.

Huma One tiny thing . . . when Blanche says, 'Let go of that broom' – would you mind if Stella is actually holding one?

Nina steals the money, goes to door, stares at Manuela, pushes past her, storms off.

Nina?

Nina is disappearing into backstage.

You know, Nina . . . I just want you to be happy.

Nina exits through the fire exit door.

Nina?

Manuela I'm not Nina. I'm Manuela.

Enter Huma from the bathroom, half-dressed.

Huma Who?
You're not meant to be in here – where did you come from? Nina?

Manuela She just left . . .

Huma What?!

She rushes out into the empty theatre. Her voice echoes.

Nina! Nina! Hello? Where's Alex?! Someone?!

Emptiness. She rushes back to the dressing room.

Where did she go, did she say anything?

Manuela No . . . she seemed in a rush.

Huma (*half screams, beside herself*) We've only been here a week. How could she? (*Notices handbag.*) Oh, Jesus. Did you see her with this?

> *Manuela shakes her head. Huma looks through the handbag.*

Damn her! (*Flings it away. Hand to face, tearfully distraught.*) And who the hell let you in?

Manuela I saw the play tonight.

Huma You and six hundred others.

Manuela And the matinee . . .

Huma Oh, one of those.

Manuela No, I . . . I love Tennessee Williams.

Huma And this production?

Manuela (*knows right answer*) Magnificent.

Huma Even with a sabotaging Stella who randomly decides there isn't a baby? (*Lights a cigarette.*) Look, what do you want? Is it an autograph, what?

Manuela No.

Huma Then why are you here?

> *Manuela can't answer that. She begins to take Esteban's notebook from her handbag. But Huma's mind is suddenly elsewhere:*

Do you know Barcelona well?

Manuela Um . . . yes.

Huma Do you have a car?

40

Manuela Why?

Huma Because I need a lift!

Manuela Where to?

Huma Junkies. Take me to the dealers, the junkies.

Manuela I think you can manage that on your own . . .

Huma I can't, I can't drive.

Manuela I'm not going to help you score, Señora Rojo.

Huma Oh, for God's sake, it's not for me – it's where I'll find *her*.

Heroin. Please don't tell anyone. Do you know where she'd go at this hour?

Manuela No . . . but it's not hard to find out.

Huma You mean you could?

A moment.

Manuela Yes.

Huma finds her magnificent cape, puts it on. Manuela helps.

Huma We'll stop at a bank, I'll pay you for your time . . .

Manuela You don't need to . . .

Huma Yes I do: this junkie stuff, it's so foreign to me: you, you translate.

In her cape, she looks as she did in Madrid. Manuela stares.

What?

Manuela Nothing.

Huma I look horrendous, I know.

Manuela You look beautiful.

Huma Where have you been all my life? Thank you, whoever you are.

Manuela Manuela.

Huma Huma.

Manuela I know.

Huma strides out of the dressing room, Manuela follows.

Huma God damn the girl . . .

Manuela We'll find her.

They walk on to the stripped-back stage. Manuela is overwhelmed by the hugeness of the theatre, looks up into the gods.

I will go with you.

Unwittingly, she has used some words of Stella's. Huma shouts into the gods:

Huma Good night, Pablo!

The working lights are switched off with an echoic click.

Hurry . . . please . . . before some lunatic pusher cuts her to bits.

The fire exit door closes behind them.

FIFTEEN

Spotlight on Agrado, in her Chanel, with the microphone.

Agrado Now, as we're descended from monkeys, irreversible laser treatment is required to remove body hair – a snip at sixty thousand pesetas a session. Speaking of the snip, the answer is no, I never wanted it, because those who've had it never get any trade. It would have been very easy to fuck up my career with a superfluous procedure: our customers like us to have pneumatic tits and large dicks –

A very loud doorbell.

(*To front row.*) No, darling, I didn't say '*rh*eumatic tits' – I'm not on the market for necrophiles – I said, '*pn*eumatic tits' – you know, boobs like inflated car tyres and a cock that goes for days.

Doorbell.

Oh, you want to see it?

Doorbell.

She wants to see it!

Spotlight out.

Honestly, Pablo, as if I would!

SIXTEEN

Doorbell rings incessantly. A framed photo of Esteban watches over Manuela, sleeping on the sofa in her living room. She wakes confusedly.

Manuela All right, all right . . . (*Answers door.*)

Sister Rosa Manuela, you're home!

Manuela Rosa.

Sister Rosa Good morning. Are you by yourself?

Manuela I've just woken up . . .

Sister Rosa It's half past eleven!

Manuela It was a long night . . .

Sister Rosa You didn't even get undressed. Back on the game . . . already. I don't believe you. After everything I did, you fall straight back in to it.

Manuela I was on the streets, but it's not what you think. How did you find me, Rosa?

Sister Rosa Agrado!

Manuela Ah . . .

Sister Rosa I'm here to say sorry.

Manuela It doesn't matter, honestly.

Sister Rosa I can't stand my mother, she can be such a – (*Registers sparsely furnished room.*) Have you just moved in?

Manuela Rosa, this isn't a good time . . . would you mind? I need / a shower –

Sister Rosa Parents can be such pains, can't they? Where are yours? Argentina?

Manuela No. Dead.

Sister Rosa So you're all alone?

Manuela I suppose that's it. Yes.

Sister Rosa Oh, Manuela. I almost envy you.

Manuela is taken aback by the girl's apparently innocent determination to make herself at home.

I've never met a whore who was also a nurse.

Manuela I'm not a whore. I've never been a whore. I've been fucked around a lot, but I'm not a whore.
It was Agrado's idea. That was her dress – I shouldn't have worn it.

Sister Rosa Do you mean you pretended to be a prostitute to try and get a job out of me at the refuge?

44

Manuela It was wrong . . . but I have to live.

Sister Rosa Could I have a glass of water?

Manuela Are you all right?

Sister Rosa A bit shaky. I need to catch my breath.

Manuela Five minutes – then I'm calling you a taxi.

She gets the water. Sister Rosa looks about, picks up photo.

Sister Rosa Who's this handsome boy?

Manuela Esteban, my son.

Sister Rosa Oh. I thought you said you were alone?

Manuela He died.
An accident.

Sister Rosa gasps, puts the photo down gently. She doesn't know what to say, holds out her hand in sympathy. Manuela gives her the water. She gulps like a child, breathlessly.

Sister Rosa You need furniture!

Manuela Yes.

Sister Rosa And company.

Manuela I like being on my own.

Sister Rosa I've just had a marvellous thought. A new plan for you to make money.

Manuela No offence, but if it's anything like the last one I'll say no now.

Sister Rosa Why don't I rent a room from you here?

Manuela What?

Sister Rosa How much would you charge?

Manuela I'm not taking money from you . . . Stop worrying about me . . . Anyway, the woman I hit the streets with last night offered me a job! (*Teasingly produces a business card from her handbag.*)

Sister Rosa What woman?

Manuela A famous one.

Sister Rosa Doing what?

Manuela PA.

Sister Rosa Sounds very dodgy, who is she? (*Snatches card.*)

Manuela What business is it / of yours? (*Takes card back.*)

Sister Rosa My aunt left me some money, I could pay *all* of your rent.

Manuela Rosa, stop it, it's not going to happen. Why do you need to move – they look after you at the refuge, don't they?

Sister Rosa Yes, but I've told them I'm going to El Salvador. I'm not.
  I'm pregnant.

Manuela is shocked. Sister Rosa nods.

Manuela Rosa . . .

She takes Rosa's hand. A moment.

Sister Rosa I've just thought . . . I could have it *here*, and there'd be much less scandal.

Manuela What are you talking about? We hardly know each other!

Sister Rosa I feel as if we do . . .

Manuela Can't the father help you?

Sister Rosa God knows where he is . . .

Manuela But you know *who* he is?

Sister Rosa Of course, what do you take me for?

Manuela Oh, forgive me, it's just, you know, I don't often meet pregnant nuns –

Sister Rosa It's Lola.

Manuela doesn't take it in.

Your fellow Argentine.
  The father is Lola.

Manuela is on her feet, beside herself, lost for words.

Manuela Lola? Lola?! That . . . that . . . *piece of fucking shit* –

Sister Rosa Manuela?

Manuela Lola??

Sister Rosa What's the / matter?

Manuela The *matter*?!

Sister Rosa I'm a bit worried.

Manuela I'm not fucking surprised!

Sister Rosa I bled a little this morning.

Manuela How far gone are you?

Sister Rosa About three months.

Manuela Then you've got to go to the doctor straight away!

Sister Rosa I'm . . . I'm scared to make an appointment.

Manuela Rosa! Are you mad? – you shouldn't be bleeding now!

Sister Rosa Will you help?
  Please. No one else knows.

Manuela Jesus Christ . . .

Sister Rosa Please stop . . .

Manuela Lola?! How . . . how?

Sister Rosa I don't know . . .
She was so sad . . . funny . . .
I sort of fell in love, I think.

Manuela can't take it, can't help but pace. Sister Rosa is very upset.

Please don't shout any more. All I hear in my head is shouting. Just help me.

Manuela That . . . fucking . . .

Sister Rosa Will you let me stay?

Manuela No, no, I'm sorry, no.

Walks out. Sister Rosa wipes away her tears. Then she notices Esteban's notebook. She picks it up innocently, opens it. Manuela returns.

Put my son's notebook down, please.

Sister Rosa obeys. A moment. She makes herself comfortable.

Sister Rosa Do you know, there's only one thing I want. Just to shut my eyes.

Manuela I'm booking you an appointment, then I'm ordering you a cab.

Sister Rosa I'd give the world for sleep.

Manuela You can, but not here.

Sister Rosa I don't know if there's a God any more.

Manuela What?

Sister Rosa All I want is to dream and keep dreaming for ever. Isn't that funny?

Manuela You have to leave.

SEVENTEEN

Manuela, Sister Rosa and a Gynaecologist, with notes.

Gynaecologist You're lucky.

Sister Rosa Oh?

Gynaecologist You should have been here weeks ago. Still . . . the foetus is fine.

Sister Rosa Thank God.

Gynaecologist With your hypertension there is a real risk of miscarriage . . . You need to rest as much as you can. Do you live together?

Sister Rosa Yes.

Manuela No.

Gynaecologist Shall we get the story straight?

Manuela We're sisters. She lives with our mother . . . but she hasn't told her yet.

Sister Rosa I can't give up my job.

Gynaecologist Your only job now is to rest and not do anything stupid. Tell your mother: rest.

Manuela I understand.

Sister Rosa Doctor?
I work with high-risk people. I'd like to have an Aids test, if possible.

Gynaecologist What do you do?

Manuela (*answers before Sister Rosa can*) Social worker.

A moment.

Gynaecologist Wait here.

Leaves. Manuela stares out front. The sea is their view through the windows.

Sister Rosa The Barceloneta looks like a postcard.

A moment. Manuela is not looking at Sister Rosa.

Manuela Stop it, Rosa.

Sister Rosa What?

Manuela Staring. You have to tell your mother. Someone has to look after you. You can't do this to me.
You were right not to say anything about the father.

Sister Rosa Why do you hate Lola so much, Manuela?

Manuela I don't. But she does have the worst of a man and the worst of a woman.
Damn those people. Damn the whole Mediterranean . . .

Sister Rosa looks at her; Manuela continues to stare out at the sea. Eventually:

I was so young when I got married. I thought it would be OK . . . then my husband decided he'd rather be in Paris. I waited for him to come home . . . Out of the blue, I got a call, 'It's all happening in Barcelona, Manuela, I'm selling paella from a shack on the beach, come to Spain, come!' So I did. He was the same . . . there were tits on his chest, but otherwise the same . . . so I ended up resigning myself to our life. Women do that. Because we're fucking idiots. (*Points.*) It was down there. It's changed now; it was incredible back then. Except while I gutted the fish and dealt with the customers, he squeezed himself into a skimpy bikini and shagged everything that moved. Of course if wifey showed any leg he went berserk. Tits and balls, a deadly combination.
Don't ask me to do this, Rosa . . . You can't stay with me . . . I'm heartless . . . there's nothing in here (*Taps chest, paces.*) God, I can't stand this hospital . . .

Sister Rosa But you were a nurse.

Manuela That's why! – I've got to / go –

Sister Rosa Manuela –

Manuela Listen: in Madrid I was a coordinator for the NTO. Transplants. I had exclusive access to donors' files. I would . . . run my finger down lists and find matches for kidneys, livers . . . bodiless bits of / life –

Sister Rosa If it was your / job –

Manuela I went through the files illegally.

Sister Rosa What?

Manuela Because I could. A criminal, I broke every rule in the fucking book. I found the man who took my son's heart, Rosa. Esteban's. I scrawled down his / details . . .

Sister Rosa Manuela –

Manuela No, shut up . . . it was madness, the stupidest thing I've done, but I couldn't help it. I found this man – Miguel – and I stalked him. I saw him the day he was discharged. He's halfway through his life; my son had lived less than a quarter of his. His mother was with him, and wife and kids . . . he had all those things, all that love – and he had my Esteban's heart. I spied on them coming out of the hospital . . . they were joking about how he could eat cheeseburgers again . . . because Esteban's blood was in his veins. I'm not fit for this; nothing means anything any more. I lost my heart, Rosa, I don't have one. It went the day Esteban lost his.

Sister Rosa remains silent as Manuela cries. And then she can't control her anger:

You've no right to ask me to be your mother. You've already got one, even if you hate her. We can't choose our parents, they are who they are.

Enter a Nurse, with notes.

Nurse María Rosa Sans?

Sister Rosa Yes?

Nurse We can do your test. This way.

Sister Rosa You mean now?

Nurse Follow me, please.

Sister Rosa Manuela . . .

Manuela No, Rosa. You'll be all right.

EIGHTEEN

Huma, nearly ready as Blanche, opens the door of her dressing room to Manuela.

Huma Manuela.

She smiles, holds out her hand; they shake.

Manuela Hello.

Huma I had a feeling you'd say yes.

Manuela Actually, I was going to say no till I rang you.

Huma What changed your mind?

A moment.

Manuela I need the money.

Huma Good. You're honest. I like that.

Enter Alex, with mail.

Alex Mail, Señora Rojo.

Huma Thank you, Alex. This is Manuela.

Alex mutters a 'Hi', then leaves.

Come in . . .

Manuela The truth is . . . I'm not that honest. You asked me to bring references. I don't have any. I lost my old job.

Huma How?

Manuela Señora Rojo –

Huma Huma, please –

Manuela I know I shouldn't be stating terms, but . . . I can't talk about my life. If that means you don't trust me, don't let me start.

Huma You found Nina in what to me looked like hell. I trust you.
   (*Hands her a diary.*) My diary. Perpetual chaos. Things are always coming in. I try politely to say no to most. Here, it's bits and pieces: messages, picking up dry cleaning, that kind of thing. And I like coffee an hour before the performance, if that's not too menial.

Manuela Of course not . . .

Huma Mostly, I need you to be . . . a confidante. Someone to talk to . . . about anything. That's what I'm really paying you for, Manuela: to listen.

Manuela Understood.

   Huma smiles. Enter Nina, in (non-pregnant) costume as Stella.

Huma Darling, you remember Manuela? She found you with your dope-pushing smackhead friends just after you pilfered all my money.

Nina Hilarious, Huma. What are you doing here?

Huma Don't play dumb, I told you before. She's decided to start immediately.

Manuela Hello, Nina.

Nina (*mimics*) Hello, Nina.

Huma For once, Nina, you're not loaded, and I'm doing something for myself. Sorry if those things are annoying.

Goes to bathroom. Nina smokes, challenges Manuela with a stare and pose.

Manuela It's been a long tour. Is it hard to keep it fresh? Where do you come from, Nina? Do you have family?

Nina You steer clear of me.

She produces a small bottle of vodka, swigs. Puts it away as Huma comes out of the bathroom.

Are you fucking her?

Huma Nina! (*To Manuela.*) I'm sorry.

Nina I'd watch myself if I were you, she's always looking for fresh muff.

She walks out.

Huma It's not true.

Manuela She'll always hate me.

Huma Nina hates everyone. (*At dressing table, puts on last of Blanche.*)

No one understands. I hear the others all the time: 'What does she see in her?'

Sometimes she crushes me, and I feel old. Then she'll say something so winning I could take off. I love her. It's that simple, Manuela. (*Lights cigarette, offers.*)

Manuela No, thanks.

Huma When I was fifteen I saw Bette Davis smoking like that – (*the poster*) and fell madly in love – with her and the fag. (*Makes to leave.*)

Manuela Do you need anything? Dinner?

Huma Cod – with salad. The restaurant on the corner, they know me.

Manuela Done.

A very loud doorbell. Huma turns back to Manuela. On the Streetcar *stage, Isabel is revealed as Eunice, Nina as Stella and Mario as Stanley; and an actress as Matron and an actor as Doctor; with, if possible, actors as poker players.*

Isabel That must be them.

Huma I don't suppose you'd be able to get some kind of sedative for her? Just to take the edge off?

Manuela I think she's already found a –
I've got Lexotan.

Huma Perfect. Who knows, you might even become friends.

Doorbell.

I'm delighted, Manuela. Thank you.

She smiles, walks out of the dressing room, stubs out cigarette, steps on stage:

NINETEEN

And Manuela is now watching Streetcar *from a new, backstage perspective:*

Blanche Is it the gentleman I was expecting from Dallas?

Isabel *as* **Eunice** I think it is, Blanche.

Blanche I'm not quite ready.

Stella Ask him to wait outside.

Eunice goes. Drums sound very softly.

Everything packed?

Blanche My silver toilet articles are still out.

Stella Ah!

Eunice (*returning*) They're waiting in front of the house.

Blanche They! Who's 'they'?

Eunice There's a lady with him.

Blanche I cannot imagine who this 'lady' could be!

Stella Shall we go, Blanche?

Blanche Must we go through that room?

Stella I will go with you.

Blanche How do I look?

Stella Lovely.

Eunice (*echoing*) Lovely.

> *They walk through the poker players, who stand awkwardly at the table.*

Blanche Please don't get up. I'm only passing through.

Actor *as* **Doctor** How do you do?

Blanche You are not the gentleman I was expecting.

> *She suddenly gasps and starts. She stops by Stella. Eunice is holding Stella's arm. The Matron advances.*

Actress *as* **Matron** Hello, Blanche.

Blanche (*retreating in panic*) I don't know you – I don't know you. I want to be – left alone – please!

Matron Now, Blanche!

She steps boldly towards Blanche. Blanche screams and tries to break past.

Stella Oh, God, oh, please, God, don't hurt her! Oh, God, what have I done to my sister?

The Matron catches hold of Blanche's arm. Blanche turns wildly and scratches. The woman pinions her arms. Blanche cries out hoarsely and slips to her knees.

Matron These fingernails have to be trimmed. Jacket, Doctor?

Doctor Not unless necessary.

He takes off his hat. His voice is gentle and reassuring as he crouches in front of Blanche.

Miss DuBois.

Blanche stares at him with desperate pleading. He smiles.

Blanche (*faintly*) Ask her to let go of me.

Doctor Let go.

The Matron releases her. Blanche extends her hands towards the Doctor. He draws her up gently.

Blanche Whoever you are – I have always depended on the kindness of strangers.

They go out.

Stella Blanche! Blanche, Blanche!

Climax, applause, and the Streetcar *company lurches forward to take its curtain call.*

TWENTY

Manuela, new hair and clothes, on the phone, in the dressing room. It feels spruced up. Enter Alex. Manuela puts the phone behind her back.

Alex You've found her? You haven't found her?

Manuela Hello again, Alex. You haven't given us the new kettle I asked for last / week –

Alex Manuela, this isn't the / time for –

Manuela Everything's fine.

Alex Then where is she? (*Into headset.*) I don't know! (*To Manuela.*) Fix this. Find her.

Exits. Manuela resumes with the phone.

Manuela Hello –?

No one there. She hangs up in frustration, presses 'redial'. Re-enter Alex.

Alex She was with some guy yesterday in the bar – perhaps she's with him?

Manuela I'm dealing with it. And don't tell Huma that!

Alex sighs, leaves.

Fuck. Answer, for God's sake . . .

Enter Huma, in Streetcar *costume.*

Huma Well?

Manuela She's not in the alley?

Huma (*shakes head*) Stage door are next to useless. I've searched everywhere.

Manuela When did you last see her?

Huma At home this morning – I've been filming all day. The car park!

Manuela In your costume?

Huma puts on an enormous pair of dark glasses, sweeps off, bumps into Alex.

Alex Huma –

Huma Out of my way, Alex.

Alex We're down to the wire.

Huma I'm aware of that.

Leaves. Alex stares at Manuela.

Manuela She just rang.

Alex Don't lie.

Manuela She's on her way. Five minutes.

Alex leaves. Manuela screams, picks up phone again.

Please, Nina . . . answer . . .

Enter Mario, in costume as Stanley.

Mario Hi, Manuela.

Manuela Hello, Mario. (*A routine.*) Here, why don't you steal one of Huma's fags?

Mario Ta. (*Lights up.*) It's much better round here since you arrived, Manuela.

Manuela Stop staring at my tits, Mario.

Enter Isabel, in costume as Eunice, with Nina, black-eyed, bloody, laughing, moaning.

Isabel Manuela!

Manuela Nina, where have you –? Oh, no . . .

Isabel I found her on the street –

Mario Ooh – nasty.

Manuela Get out.

Mario leaves. Nina laughs pointedly, sways on her feet.

Oh, Nina, what are you up to? Five minutes before curtain?

Isabel She's been on the end of a fist.

Manuela Someone beat you?

Nina slumps into a chair, cries, nods, thuds her head on the dressing table.

Oh, Nina . . . it's all right . . . not here . . . Isabel, I don't want to upset Huma. (*To Nina.*) We won't tell her yet, OK? Quickly . . .

They help her to the bathroom. Enter Huma, hysterical, smoking.

Huma She's not there, I'm going to kill – Manuela? Manuela!

Manuela eases herself out of the bathroom.

Manuela Here I am.

Huma No sign.

Manuela Don't panic, Huma.

Enter Alex.

Alex Manuela / I –

Huma Did I say you could enter? Why do you keep looking at me as if it's my fault? I've spent the whole day on location, I haven't seen her.

Alex Mario / said –

Huma And why do you keep bringing the curtain down so early? We could have taken at least one more bow last night!

Alex Mario said she's here. She's ready to go, right? (*Looks around.*)

Manuela Everything's all right, Huma. (*Gives her a meaningful look.*)

Alex She needs to get into costume.

Manuela She can't.

Alex Why?

Manuela Food poisoning.

Huma Is she all right?

Manuela It's not serious. That restaurant you go to. The cod.

Alex Manuela, we really don't have time for this crap –

Manuela It isn't crap – it's gastroenteritis.

Alex Did she call the doctor?

Manuela Of course. He told her to drink fluids and stay in bed but she decided to give it her best shot, which was committed of her, don't you think? Now she's paying for it.

Alex And where does this leave tonight?

Huma Why won't the producers employ understudies? Bloody cheapskates!

Manuela I'd like to speak to Huma. Give us a moment?

Huma Get out, Alex, and if you come in uninvited again I'll have you fired.

Alex leaves.

What?

Manuela Please don't be upset, Huma.

Huma What?

Isabel, trying to stop Nina at the bathroom door.

Isabel Nina . . .

Huma Nina? Oh, God . . . my darling.

Nina (*collapses into her arms*) Huma . . .

Manuela helps guide her to a chair.

Huma You're safe here. You're safe now, my sweet girl. (*Caresses her.*) What have you done? Shhh . . . shhh . . .

Manuela You mustn't worry. (*Sees to Nina's wound.*)

Huma What happened?

Isabel Um, she's off her face.

Manuela It's a graze, isn't it, Nina? She just needs to sleep it off.

Huma Silly girl. Silly, silly girl. What are we going to do?

Isabel Mario saw her.

Huma She's on such thin ice.

A moment.

Manuela I could help.
  I could play Stella.

Huma What?

Manuela I know it. I've listened to it for two weeks. I think it's gone in.

Alex (*outside door, knocks*) Huma?

Huma You?

Alex Are we opening the house?!

Manuela I think I could manage it . . . if you wanted.

Huma Can you act?

Manuela Well, I'm quite a good liar. And I know how to improvise. My son used to say I was a very good actress.

Huma Your son?

Alex We're all waiting! Huma! Is she or isn't she?

Manuela and Huma regard each other.

Manuela Only if it would help, Huma. It's up to you.

A moment. Huma opens the door.

Huma Delay the curtain by half an hour.

Alex But –

Huma Do it. (*Closes it. To Manuela.*) Have you got any friends you want to come in?

Manuela laughs.

It's really not funny.

Manuela It's really not.

Huma You're sure you know it?

Manuela (*sorry to say that she does*) Yes.

Huma Put her in her dressing room, Isabel. I'll sort things out with Alex.

Manuela (*at door, looks out*) All clear.

Isabel Come on, Nina . . .

Leaves with Nina.

Huma Use my make-up . . .
Try to upstage me, my darling, and I will eat you for supper.

Leaves after Isabel and Nina. Manuela is on her own. She puffs at her face. She begins to de-Manuela by arranging her hair as Stella. She mumbles her way through a line.

Manuela 'She married a boy who wrote poetry . . . I think Blanche didn't just love him, but worshipped the ground he walked on!'

During this, backstage comes to silent, industrious life. Crew ready props and furniture. Streetcar *walls and scrims descend. Enter Sister Rosa through the fire exit door in the back wall. She has a small handbag. Though out of place, she is inconspicuous in the activity. She traverses the landscape as Manuela did. Alex comes into the dressing room.*

Alex Everyone thinks I hate her. I just want her to not get shit-faced and do her job.
   You can't be serious about this?

Manuela I just want to help, Alex.

A moment.

Alex I'll cue every entrance. Don't take your eyes off me.

Manuela nods. Alex leaves, crashing into Sister Rosa in the corridor. Manuela continues:

Manuela 'But then she found out this talented and beautiful –' *beautiful* and *talented* – 'young man was a degenerate –'

Sister Rosa knocks. Alex charges back in:

Alex So you know, Huma will lose her rag if you go anti-clockwise round that fucking / table.

Manuela Rosa?

Sister Rosa Hello, Manuela.

Manuela What are you doing here? You shouldn't be out.

Alex Señorita, this way . . .

Sister Rosa shakes her head.

Manuela Give us a second, Alex? My costumes?

Alex I don't even know your surname.

Manuela Echevarría.

Exit Alex.

Rosa . . . I can't talk now . . . I'm sorry . . . shouldn't you be in bed? You shouldn't have come here.

Sister Rosa You don't remember. (*Produces an envelope.*) My appointment.

She hands Manuela the envelope. Manuela opens it, reads. After what seems like an eternity, she looks to Sister Rosa.

I'm HIV positive.

Manuela (*screws paper up*) We'll do another test.

Sister Rosa There's no need.

Manuela What the fucking hell were you thinking when you screwed Lola? She's been shooting up for fifteen years – you knew that! What world are you living in, Rosa?

Sister Rosa cries. Manuela's eyes are ablaze with anger.

Sister Rosa I don't know.

Manuela What world?!

An announcement is suddenly broadcast in the theatre:

Announcement Ladies and gentlemen. This evening's performance of *A Streetcar Named Desire* will be delayed by half an hour. Due to the indisposition of Señorita Nina Cruz, the role of Stella Kowalski will be played at this performance by her . . . understudy . . . (*Rustle of paper.*) Señora Manuela Echevarría.

Sister Rosa Manuela?

Manuela Don't ask.

She doesn't know whether to laugh or cry. Sister Rosa cries.

Rosa . . .

They hug.

Have you told your mother?

Sister Rosa No.

Manuela The other nuns?

Sister Rosa shakes her head.

You can move in with me. You can move in with me.

Sister Rosa breaks down in gratitude. They hug and cry.

I just have to do this one thing, Rosa. Wait for me – I'll ring Agrado, she'll come and be with you this evening – but don't tell her anything. OK?

Sister Rosa nods.

Stay and watch . . . and then I'll take you home. It will be all right, Rosa. Listen: I will never leave you. I swear to you.

Enter Alex, with Nina's costumes.

Alex Twenty-five minutes, Señora Echevarría. And frankly they're a fucking tough crowd.

Sister Rosa looks to Manuela questioningly. Overwhelmed by the sheer madness and tragedy of it all, the women burst into laughter, their hands to their tear-stained cheeks.

TWENTY-ONE

Manuela steps into a bare space, takes off her dress.
Huma and Isabel help her on with the Stella dress, with
its pregnancy stomach. Manuela breathes heavily. Alex
hands her a birthday cake ablaze with lighted candles.
Then she is alone.

Manuela Blanche? Blanche?

TWENTY-TWO

Manuela *as* **Stella** Blanche?

> *A new-found electricity energises all the* Streetcar
> *performances.*

Blanche Oh, those pretty, pretty little candles! You
ought to save them for baby's birthdays. Oh, I hope
candles are going to glow in his life and I hope that
his eyes are going to be like candles, like two blue
candles lighted in a white cake!

Stanley What poetry!

Blanche His auntie knows candles aren't safe, that
candles burn out in little boys' and girls' eyes, or
wind blows them out and after that happens,
electric light bulbs go on and you see too plainly . . .

Stanley Sister Blanche, I've got a little birthday
remembrance for you.

Blanche Oh, have you, Stanley? I wasn't expecting
any, I – I don't know why Stella wants to observe
my birthday! When you – reach twenty-seven! Well –
age is a subject that you'd prefer to – ignore! What
is it? Why, why – Why, it's a –

Stanley Ticket! On the Greyhound! Tuesday!

TWENTY-THREE

The entire company – and the All About My Mother *crew – emerge from places all around the theatre to watch Manuela. Agrado and Sister Rosa are audience, as Esteban and Manuela were once before. Manuela plays with more raw emotion than Nina.*

Stella You didn't need to do that. You needn't have been so cruel.

Stanley Delicate piece she is.

Stella She is. She was. You didn't know Blanche as a girl. Nobody was tender and trusting as she was. But people like you abused her, and forced her to change. Why did you do this to her?

Stanley I done nothing to no one. Let go of my shirt. You've torn it.

Stella I want to know why.

Stanley When we first met, you thought I was common . . . and how you loved it . . . ! Wasn't we happy together? Wasn't it all OK? Till she showed here?

Manuela-Stella feels the child inside her, and it provokes grief.

Hoity-toity, describing me as an ape.

The pregnant Manuela-Stella is sobbing. Her body gives way; she is on the ground.

Hey, what is it, Manuela . . .

Mario, stunned by the rawness of Manuela's performance, is a little confused.

. . . Stella?

Stella Take me to the hospital.

Manuela-Stella is sobbing uncontrollably. Mario-Stanley takes her offstage.

TWENTY-FOUR

And, backstage, people rush to Manuela as the onstage action continues with Huma-Blanche's entrance. But Huma-Blanche doesn't sing. She stares at the blazing candles on the cake. She blows them out. It washes stage light over Esteban, standing over his grieving mother, then house lights over the All About My Mother *audience.*

Act Two

ONE

Spotlight on Esteban, with the microphone.

Esteban Spanish translates it as *Eva Laid Bare*, but the title is *All About Eve*. In the movie, Eve Harrington, played by Anne Baxter, waits at the stage door of the theatre where Bette Davis is acting in a play. Someone lets Eve in . . . but what no one realises is that she's a pushy actress: the second she enters the dressing room, she's destined to become a star and wipe the floor with Bette Davis. At first, I saw Mama like that . . . but then I thought about her reading to me . . . or stroking a patient's hand . . . or just waiting for someone who's running late. Mama isn't ambitious. In *my* story, my character is drawn into the dressing room of the famous Spanish actress Huma Rojo – but unlike Eve she makes herself crucial to the people she meets.

I'm shaking things up, making them my own.

He puts microphone down, retreats from spotlight.

TWO

Nina, pacing the dressing room, barking at Huma.

Huma She says she learnt it over the Tannoy.

Nina That's a pile of shit!

Huma Calm down.

Nina Don't tell me to calm down, I'm completely fucking serene, actually.

Huma Have a cigarette.

Nina Yeah, right, your answer to all life's problems: drugs!

Huma Did you just make a joke, Nina? (*Laughs affectionately, caresses her.*)

Nina Huma . . . stop . . . I'm serious . . . it's weird . . .

Huma kisses her, they cuddle. Enter Manuela, with dry cleaning.

Manuela Hello . . .

Nina Oh, and here she is: the little starlet, bang on time.

Manuela I'm sorry?

Nina Pure as the driven fucking snow.

Manuela Your dry cleaning, Huma . . .

Nina Jesus, she makes me want to throw up.

Enter Alex, with mail.

Alex Evening, all. Oh, hello, Nina. Still got salmonella? There's mail for you, Manuela.

Gives it to her, leaves.

Nina Fan mail?! Bloody fan mail?!

Manuela I'll come back later . . .

Nina Don't go: there are casting directors in tonight. We can see through you.

Manuela Stop it, Nina.

Nina Fuck off.

Huma Nina, that's enough. There's no need to be rude.

Nina The Tannoy? You expect us to believe that? You learnt it deliberately!

Manuela No. The Tannoy helped me . . . but I already knew it.

I've known the part of Stella for years.

Nina Really? How convenient! So you didn't just stroll into Huma's dressing room one night for absolutely no reason?

Manuela There was a reason.

Nina I knew it!

Manuela I have to go –

Nina Who are you, Miss Echevarría?

Manuela Let me get my things . . .

Nina Fuck you, fuck off – what the fuck is your game?

A moment.

Huma Manuela. I think you owe us an explanation.

Nina and Huma watch her. Yet again Manuela tries to leave; Nina blocks the way. She is cornered. She can hardly find the words.

Manuela *A Streetcar Named Desire* . . . has marked my life.

Twenty years ago . . . I was in an amateur company. I played Stella. It's where I met my husband . . . he played Stanley. Two months ago I saw you when you were in Madrid. I took my son . . . it was his birthday. We waited for you outside the theatre because he wanted your autograph . . . It was pouring with rain, but he'd got it into his head . . . he wouldn't move . . .

Esteban Señora Rojo?!

Manuela It was stupid . . . we were soaked . . . but it was his birthday . . . I couldn't . . . I couldn't . . . (*Takes photo from her handbag.*) Here he is.

Esteban Wait, Señora Rojo!

Huma doesn't dare touch the photograph, stares, gasps involuntarily.

Manuela My son, Esteban. (*To* Nina, *chokes on grief.*) You walked off –

Esteban Señora Rojo!

Manuela – disappeared into the rain. He ran across the street without . . . A car ploughed into him . . . He was on the road . . . I think of him, and I see him there . . . I don't remember anything except . . . my hands in his blood . . . and that he'd chased you, Huma.
So here I am.
Your explanation.

Leaves. Huma *stares after her. Ever the professional, she begins to put on Blanche.*

Nina Huma?
I don't remember.
Huma?

Huma Rain. I heard something, it hit me here (*the gut*). But you were in a vile mood and you'd rushed off around the corner . . . so I followed you . . . like I always do. (*Re. make-up.*) You too, Nina.

Nina I never wanted this.

Huma What?

Nina To be an actor. It's not me. I'm no good at it.

Huma Shhh. Sit next to me.

Nina Huma . . .

Huma Please.
Shall we go somewhere on Sunday?

Nina cries. Huma *lets it happen.*

Put your face on. It won't do it by itself.
    There's my girl.

THREE

Spotlight on Agrado, in her Chanel, with the microphone.

Agrado Of course instead of totting up the cost of my
work, I could simply elongate my vowels and give you
my Blanche DuBois. I'm perfect for it, you know, in age
if nothing else; I'm only forty, though I feel much older.
I've myself to blame for that: hundreds of men have beaten
the living shit out of me, but it's nothing compared to the
beating I've given myself. Yes, ladies and gentlemen, for a
real Blanche, optimistic on the outside and ravaged
within, look no further:

    I have always depended –

Doorbell.

    I have always –

Doorbell.

    – depended on the kindness –

Spotlight out.

Bitch!

FOUR

*Doorbell. Sister Rosa with a half-finished plate of lunch,
at Manuela's.*

Sister Rosa That's Agrado!

Manuela How do you know that? You didn't tell her
anything, did you?

Sister Rosa shakes her head, unconvincingly.

Rosa?

Sister Rosa Just that I might be here today . . .

Manuela No!

Sister Rosa She was so annoyed I knew all about *Streetcar* before she did – she kept interrogating me!

Doorbell.

Manuela Ignore it.

Sister Rosa But, Manuela –

Manuela We're not at home. You can't have visitors today.

Sister Rosa I feel fine!

Manuela Rosa. Stop arguing. Have you finished?

Sister Rosa nods.

Do you want ice cream?

Sister Rosa nods. Manuela disappears to the kitchen. Sister Rosa pauses, then opens the door to Huma.

Sister Rosa Oh.

Huma Hello.

Sister Rosa Hello.

Huma Does Manuela live here?

Sister Rosa Yes.

Huma My name is Huma.

Sister Rosa I know. I saw you on stage the night before last.

Huma You did?

Sister Rosa Yes!

Huma And?

Sister Rosa Wasn't Manuela a star?

Not the right answer.

Huma Aren't you a sweet girl?
   Is she at home?

Enter Manuela, with a bowl of ice cream. She stares at Huma.

Hello.

Manuela Um . . . Huma . . .
   This is –

Sister Rosa Rosa.

Manuela My sister. (*Gives her bowl.*) Eat this somewhere else. Actually, go to bed.

Sister Rosa There's nothing wrong with me today.

Manuela Go.

Sister Rosa obeys unwillingly.

Sorry . . . she's like a little girl. What are you doing here, Huma?

Huma I owe you money. You left yesterday without taking your pay cheque.

Manuela You don't owe me anything.

Huma You're the best employee I've ever had.
   May I smoke?

Manuela (*shakes head*) My sister . . . isn't well . . .

Huma I wish you hadn't left like that, Manuela. I forgot my lines . . . I couldn't sleep . . . I couldn't stop thinking about your son.

Manuela I told you the day I started . . . I can't . . .

Huma (*nods*) I should have respected that.
Nina and I want you to come back.

Manuela Nina doesn't want me back.

Huma She does. We need you.

Manuela I can't leave Rosa . . .

Huma She doesn't look ill.

Manuela She is. I'm sorry if I've let you down.

Huma Manuela . . . I don't know what to do.

Manuela Get Nina into rehab! Take her out of the play.

Huma I can't . . .

Manuela Find someone to replace her, there are other actresses.

Huma I'm too tired for all that: it's Nina or no one. (*Lights up, despite Manuela's ruling.*) We've got five more months . . . God knows what then . . . They've asked me to do a Lorca . . .
Please come back.

Doorbell. Sister Rosa rushes in to get it.

Manuela Rosa, no.

Sister Rosa Visitor!

Manuela I mean it.

Sister Rosa (*looks through spy hole*) Agrado!

Manuela Shhh, come over here and sit down. Quickly.

Sister Rosa is pleased enough with that, rushes to sofa, makes herself comfortable. Doorbell. Three women pretending not to be at home. Sister Rosa giggles.

Sister Rosa Poor Agrado.

A moment.

Huma What's wrong with you, exactly?

Sister Rosa An accident.

Manuela Shush.

Doorbell. A moment.

Huma What sort?

A moment. Huma stubs out her cigarette.

Manuela I'm such an idiot!

Sister Rosa What?

Manuela Agrado could work for you.

Sister Rosa Good idea!

Huma Agrado being the person you're hiding from?

Sister Rosa We have reasons for it.

Manuela She's perfect for you, though!

Doorbell. Manuela answers the door.

Agrado Manolita! I *knew* you were home! (*Sees Huma, gasps.*) Huma. (*To Manuela.*) Huma.

Manuela Go on then, she's flesh and blood.

Huma can't believe what she sees.

Huma . . . this is Agrado.

Agrado Enchanted. I'm more than a groupie, more than a fan, I'm a groupiefan.

Huma How do you do?

Agrado Goddess, living legend. And my Manolita got to breathe your air! Bitch!

She and Manuela bark and peck as before. Huma is amazed.

We had tears running down our faces, didn't we, sister?

Sister Rosa Yes.

Agrado You're looking relaxed, for a bride of Christ.

Sister Rosa Yes!

Agrado South America's still on hold, then? This one was off to the Third World, Señora Rojo. But she's changed her mind. (*To Manuela.*) Did you know that?

Manuela shakes her head innocently.

Squeezed it out of her at *Streetcar*. And there I was, all ready to follow her to a war-torn land.

Sister Rosa I'm staying here now.

Agrado Here?

Sister Rosa At Manuela's!

Agrado Well! (*To Manuela.*) Do you know she's not going to El Salvador or don't you, you cow? Every time I talk to you, Sister Rosa, mysteries deepen. I'm not having it. What's going on?

Manuela Are you still looking for work?

Agrado Who's asking?

Huma (*demurs, wary of Agrado*) Manuela / I –

Manuela (*ignores her, continuing to Agrado*) How would you like to take over at the theatre?

Agrado You're leaving?

Manuela Yes.

Agrado Why?

Manuela Stop asking questions – do you want it or don't you?

Agrado I couldn't. I'm not a Stella, I'm a Blanche. 'Stella, my silver toilet articles are still out . . .'

Manuela I meant replace *me*, not Nina – much less Huma!

Agrado Oh. Reality bites.

Huma Manuela, I don't really / think –

Manuela I wouldn't suggest it if / I didn't –

Huma Thank you / but –

Manuela Oh, Huma, just do it. The lot of you . . . I'm sealing it with a drink! Sweet Jesus, I haven't drunk for months. This is my flat: look at you all! I'm getting some bubbly and I want you to pour it down my fucking throat!

She laughs, releasing something. The others stare at her. She exits to the kitchen.

Agrado Who died and made her the Queen of Bitches?

Sister Rosa She just wants to dump you on Huma . . .

Agrado I might not want to be dumped on Huma.

Huma Huma might not want to be dumped on. (*Makes to leave.*)

Sister Rosa Wait!
   She gives good value. They don't call her 'pleasure' for nothing.

Agrado D'you mind? (*To Huma.*) It's true. I've devoted my life to pleasing people.

Huma But 'Agrado' isn't your real name?

Agrado No, a stage name – like 'Huma'.

Huma *Touché.*

Manuela enters with a bottle and glasses.

Manuela Who's going and who's staying?

A moment.

Huma Allow me.

She takes the bottle from Manuela, pops the cork. Sister Rosa claps.

Manuela Not for you.

Sister Rosa My ice cream!

She rushes out to get it, singing. Huma pours.

Without your love,
It's a honky-tonk parade!
Without your love, /
It's a melody played
In a penny arcade!

Huma I really can't stay.

Manuela I know. Your matinee. One drink.

Huma Stunning girl, but she knows how to kill a tune.

Sister Rosa returns with her ice cream, finishes her song, curtsies.

Manuela *Brava!*

Sister Rosa Ice cream, Agrado?

Agrado You have it, you're thin as a rake. (*Suspicions mounting.*) Why can't you drink?

Manuela Cheers!

Huma Cheers!

Agrado Manuela-Stella!

All Manuela-Stella!

Sister Rosa Oh, Huma, I adored you, you were more Blanche than Blanche –

Agrado And you look so gorgeous in everything . . . that red-wine dress!

Huma It's a problem, actually . . . everything suits me.

Agrado Ditto.

Huma My tastes are catholic.

Agrado Really? Catholic?

Huma You could bottle your cheek and sell it.

Agrado My cheek is on the house.

Sister Rosa I think nuns should wear clothes like Blanche DuBois.

Agrado So you are still a nun?

Manuela (*to Huma, re. Agrado*) Try her for one day –

Agrado Stop changing the subject!

Sister Rosa Actually, I think nuns should wear Prada.

Huma's mobile rings. She looks at the caller ID.

Huma Excuse me.

Manuela Of course. Make yourself at home.

Huma removes herself. Sister Rosa giggles, picks up glass.

Sister Rosa Did you see how quickly she said yes to a drink! Mother's milk!

Manuela Shhh –

Sister Rosa I bet that's her other half, wondering where she's got to.

Manuela Calm down . . .

Sister Rosa Nina, the old ball and chain!

Manuela Stop it / now –

Agrado Both of you stop it!

Manuela What?

Sister Rosa What?

Agrado It's revolting how success has gone to your head. Acting like an actress, treating me like one of the herd. Something is up. Never forget who it was who brought you two together.

Manuela I'll tell you tomorrow, I promise.

Sister Rosa Please don't, she's so indiscreet.

Enter Huma, unnoticed.

Agrado I am not! Aren't you noticing my English-lady-sitting-on-a-carrot routine? Discretion is my middle name. I'm even discreet when I'm sucking cock. I've sucked thousands in public and aside from the recipient, no one noticed a thing.

Huma I haven't sucked a cock for forty years.

A moment. Then peals of laughter.

Sister Rosa I sucked one quite recently!

Which brings the hilarity to a close. Sister Rosa has mortified herself and shocked Manuela and Agrado.

Agrado Sister?

A moment.

Sister Rosa You need something to eat . . .

Manuela It's all right . . .

Agrado Don't worry, / we're –

Sister Rosa Yes, yes, yes, I'm making something . . . leave me / alone –

And in the embarrassed kerfuffle, a glass is knocked and smashed. Sister Rosa rushes out.

Agrado What?

Manuela Nothing.

Agrado Manuela –

Manuela Agrado: nothing.
I won't be a moment . . . (*Takes Agrado's hand.*) You and Huma talk.

She leaves after Sister Rosa. Agrado watches after her. A moment.

Huma I don't see the family similarity.

Agrado Hmm?

Huma Sisters.

Agrado Who?

Huma Manuela and Rosa.

Agrado Really?

Huma According to Manuela.

Agrado Well, if Manuela says so.

Huma I think the three of you are full of shit.

Agrado You just have to get to know us.
Is everything all right at home?

Huma nods, smiles. Agrado makes to top up their glasses. Huma shakes her head.

Huma I shouldn't have started. I like to go on stage sober.

Agrado Birds of a feather, Huma: so do I.

Huma I'm gagging for a cigarette.

Agrado offers her one. They light up, Agrado lighting her cigarette from Huma's. Esteban sits next to Huma.

So, Agrado.

Agrado Yes, goddess?

Huma Can you sew?

Agrado Naturally. I am my own couturier.

Huma Can you drive?

Agrado I used to be a lorry driver.

Huma Is that so?

Agrado In Paris, before the tits.

Huma I see.
Oh, I nearly forgot. (*Takes an envelope from her handbag, addresses Esteban directly.*) This is for you.

Esteban takes it.

Can you make good coffee?

Agrado Caffeine's been my only drug for twenty years.

Huma After *Streetcar*, depending on Nina, I might take *Blood Wedding*. Will you tour with us?

Agrado Lorca is in your blood, touring is in mine. My God, Huma, I'm done in, it's the most gruelling interview of my career.

Huma I think we've covered everything.

Agrado Good.

Huma I have to go.

Agrado And I have to take you there. Because I'm dying to meet your Nina and I just know we're going to get on like a house on fire.

They smile.

Manuela!

Enter Manuela, followed by a hangdog Sister Rosa.

Huma Thank you.

Manuela Hail Huma a cab, Agrado.

Agrado No need. My carriage awaits.

Manuela Oh! Perfect.

Huma Goodbye . . .

Manuela Goodbye, Huma . . .

They kiss as Agrado says goodbye to Sister Rosa.

Agrado Now you listen to me. Whatever's going on . . . I'd still kill to be you.

She kisses her twice, then Manuela.

Huma Why did you throw in lorry driving?

Agrado To become a whore.

Huma How interesting.

Agrado Very.

They leave.

Sister Rosa They're made for each other.

Manuela I want you to spend the rest of the day lying down.

Sister Rosa I made a fool of myself . . .

Manuela We all got carried away. You can tell people, Rosa . . . but you'll lose people when you do . . . I don't mean Agrado . . . but let's wait till the time's right.

She sits on the sofa, indicating that Sister Rosa should do the same. Sister Rosa puts her head on Manuela's shoulder.

Sister Rosa It's so lovely to be home.

She closes her eyes. Esteban hands Manuela Huma's envelope.

Esteban This is for you.

Manuela opens the envelope. Sister Rosa opens her eyes.

Sister Rosa What's that?

Manuela A cheque, from Huma. Two hundred thousand pesetas. For two weeks' work.

Sister Rosa How generous.
There's a note . . .

Manuela reads.

Esteban 'Dear Esteban. Here's the autograph you never received from me, though not because you didn't try . . .'

Manuela (*with difficulty, for Sister Rosa*) 'Dear Esteban . . .'

Sister Rosa (*takes Manuela's hand*) Yes, Manuela. I see.

FIVE

Esteban puts a blanket over Sister Rosa and makes the sofa up as a bed for her.

Sister Rosa When I was little my favourite place in the whole of Barcelona was Medinaceli Square. My father used to take me there to play. I felt safe. We'd stand on opposite sides of the fountain with the nymphs and shout to each other; we had a special game. But one day Papa just forgot how to play it, and now it's strange, but I've forgotten it too.

Esteban On Rosa's face.

Sister Rosa Rosa's nose!

Esteban On Rosa's feet.

Sister Rosa Rosa's toes!

Esteban Then what happened? Rosa knows.

Sister Rosa (*corrects*) No, no, no, it was, 'Then what happened, do you suppose?'

Esteban Then what happened, do you suppose?

Sister Rosa Rosa's toes became her nose.

Esteban And Rosa's nose?

Sister Rosa It's now her toes!
   Everything was unconfused for Papa then. And for Mama.
   Remember?

She is now very pregnant. Esteban puts a bowl of water and a flannel by her bedside. Sister Rosa sleeps.

SIX

Sister Rosa's Mother, staring at her tearfully.

Mother Rosa?
   Rosa?

Enter Manuela, with tea. Mother stares at her.

Manuela Please . . . sit down.

Mother I've never known what she's going to do next. She'd never shown any interest in religion: suddenly, she had the call. She didn't know what a prostitute was: she chooses to join the one Order the Pope's never heard of so she can be with them every day. Her whole life . . . surprise after surprise.

Manuela Will you have some tea?

Mother For God's sake, look at her.
  Tell me this is the worst of it.

Manuela Señora –

Mother Will she leave the Order? Bring it up by herself?

Manuela None of that matters now . . . She just needs rest.

Mother But something's wrong, isn't it? Or you wouldn't have rung.

Manuela I rang because you're her mother. I don't believe she can so easily block you out of her life.

Mother She's not expecting me . . .

Manuela I didn't say anything.

Mother You seem like a good sort of person . . . but I don't understand . . . why is she in this dreadful room?

Manuela She likes the view . . .

Mother And there I was, sick with worry, thinking she'd been murdered in El Salvador. So many lies.

Sister Rosa I didn't know how to tell you, Mama.

Mother Rosa . . .

Manuela Let me pour you some tea.

Mother You've done more than enough.
  Thank you.

  Manuela leaves.

Why am I always the last to know everything, Rosa?

Sister Rosa You're not.

Mother You're eight months' pregnant – and I have to find out through that woman?

Sister Rosa Her name's Manuela. And I don't know what I would have done without her.

Mother Will you get married?

Sister Rosa Mama, what sort of a question is that?

Mother A reasonable one. Who's the father?

A moment. Sister Rosa moves, flinches.

What?

Sister Rosa Cushion.
Talk to me about Papa. Is he well?

Mother The same. If it's all right with you, I won't tell him about this; he'd never understand, anyway.

Sister Rosa You didn't have to come here.

Mother Rosa . . . please tell me what I should do.

Sister Rosa Nothing.

Mother Let me do something, for pity's sake . . .

Sister Rosa It's not that I don't want help – it's just that I don't want things to become more difficult than they already are.

Mother You should wear some make-up.

Sister Rosa (*laughs weakly*) Why?

Mother Because you're such a pretty girl.

Sister Rosa sleeps. Mother watches. Enter Manuela.

I'm not blind, Manuela. What's wrong?

Manuela *Placenta preavia.* She'll need a Caesarean, when it's time. Till then . . . complete rest . . .

Mother Should I take her home with me?

Manuela You're her / mother –

Mother You know about her father's dementia . . . I have to clean him, put food to his mouth –

Manuela – you're her mother, señora, but I think she's better off here.

Mother If you need money, let me know.

Manuela nods.

Stay with her. I can see myself out.
   I don't know what I did wrong. I find her so strange. I've never known her.
   Do you have any children?

Manuela Yes, a son.

Mother Do you get on with him?

Manuela He died.

A moment.

Mother Keep me informed.
   Goodbye.

Leaves. Manuela weeps.

Sister Rosa Why did you ring her?

Manuela picks up the flannel left by Esteban and washes her, gently manipulating her inanimate body with the skill of a nurse.

Manuela Because she gave birth to you, Rosa.
   Because you love her.
   I wish it was just us . . . I wish we had no commitments to nuns or families or friends; just you and me and your baby boy, Rosa, the three of us; I wish that more than anything. But it's not how things are: there's a world, you have family.

Sister Rosa I'm going to name him Esteban.

Manuela Shhh.

Sister Rosa He'll be the third Esteban.

Manuela stops flannelling her. A moment.

My baby Esteban, your Esteban, and Lola. Our children's father.

Manuela (*stares*) Lola doesn't know we had a son. I never told him.

Sister Rosa What? But what about Esteban? He knew?

Manuela (*almost breaks, shakes head*) It's why I'm here – it's why we know each other.

A moment.

Sister Rosa This boy will belong to both of us.

SEVEN

Nina, in the semi-dark dressing room, wearing bra and knickers, taking a heroin fix, i.e. 'chasing the dragon' by heating a dose inside a strip of tinfoil and inhaling the fumes. Enter Agrado via the just-coming-to-life backstage area with a bouquet of roses. She unlocks the dressing-room door, enters, switches on light.

Agrado Nina, you scared the life –! You can't do that here!

Nina (*re. roses*) Are they for me?

Agrado It's seven o'clock, Huma will be here / soon!

Nina Where's she been today?

Agrado Out.

Nina I've been waiting, it's boring.

Agrado How did you score, anyway –? (*Suddenly mother hen.*) Oh, my darling, what's happened to your rack? You're as flat as fried eggs.

Nina Gina Lollo-fucking-brigida is flat when you're around, Agrado.

Agrado That's a lie, I'm scientifically designed to proportion.

Nina starts to prepare again.

You think I'm joking? Give that to me.

Nina No. No! (*Becomes overwrought.*) We all have our thing, you know . . .

Agrado All right –

Nina I have to . . . I *want* to . . . You don't understand . . .

Agrado It's no better up in your bubble of nothing than down here with the rest of us, Nina . . . but I'll never convince you of that.

Nina Huma should have been with me today. What's she up to?

Agrado Ever thought of having a conversation with clothes on?

She holds out a Streetcar *dress. Nina snatches it, then heaves up her breasts provocatively. Agrado responds in kind; they compare.*

Nina Show me your dick.

Agrado You can't do this shit in here.

Nina Then I'll do it in my dressing room. Tell Huma.

Agrado Get rid of it.

Nina Fine.
Excuse me? D'you mind?

93

That is, she wants privacy to get dressed. Agrado leaves with a sigh, and disappears into the theatre. Nina looks at the drugs, drops dress, prepares for another fix. Mario knocks.

Mario Agrado?

Nina (*sotto voce*) Shit . . .

Mario Agrado . . .?

Nina gathers drugs, tiptoes to bathroom. Mario opens the door, comes in. Noses about, whistles, steals a cigarette, lights up. Agrado returns with a packet of coffee.

Hello, Agrado.

Agrado Well . . . if it isn't alpha male. What are you up to?

Mario Just sneaking a crafty fag.

Agrado One of Huma's? (*Prepares coffee.*)

Mario I miss Manuela. She used to bring food in for us. Wanna go down on me?
I'm tense.

Agrado I'm tense too, Mario: why don't *you* blow *me*?

Mario It'd be the first time I've sucked a woman's dick, but if that's what it takes.

Agrado Why is this company so fixated on my dick? Mine's not the only one in the theatre, is it? You've got one, have you?

Mario Yeah.

Agrado So, you're having a quick fag in the street, do people randomly ask you to suck their dicks 'cause you've got a dick? Hmm?

Mario No.

Agrado Right, we've got an hour before you start imitating Brando again, Mario, so I'll go down on you, 'cause I'm a woman who's attuned to the needs of others, very sensitive to male tension . . . I'm going to blow you, Mario, I'm going to blow you like you're a big brass tuba.

Mario Great. That'd be . . . great.

Enter Huma, elegantly dressed. Agrado is delighted to see her.

Huma Get out, Mario.

Mario ambles out. Agrado holds out the roses excitedly. A moment.

With a blade that stops at the black root of a scream, the two men killed each other in the name of love.

I've waited my whole life to say that line.

Agrado And soon you'll be saying it every night.

Huma I once thought I'd kill to play her. (*Ignores roses, lights cigarette.*)
I turned it down.
They won't let Nina be in it. I asked them to cast her as the bride.

Agrado You're not serious?

Huma I can't do it without her, Agrado. Those were my terms.
Don't look at me like that.

A moment. Agrado throws the roses down furiously.

Agrado *Blood Wedding* is your play. Nina? You've got more talent in your toenails. Yeah, she might get somewhere if she put her mind to it . . . she's still young, quite attractive. But she won't, Huma, because she's screwed up. Ring the producers back, accept it. This is

Lorca: *you're* the one who was born for it! It's beyond that cute little junkie of yours, and you fucking know it!

Huma stares at her. Agrado holds her gaze.

Huma No one's ever spoken to me like that before.

Agrado Fine, fire me.

She lights a cigarette. They smoke.

Full house again tonight.

Huma It's a Saturday.

Agrado No, they want to see your Blanche before she's gone – what the fuck's got into you?

A moment. It takes everything Huma has to give in.

Huma All right, you're right, I'll say yes without her! Go and get something alcoholic to put in that damn coffee.

Agrado Yes, Huma.

Huma And come back and tidy up in here, it's a dump.

Agrado Then shall I lick your pussy?

Huma So vulgar.

Agrado But sweet.

Barks and leaves. Huma sits at the mirror, stares. She takes out her mobile phone, dials. Nina comes out of the bathroom, from where she has heard it all, approaches slowly. Huma sees her in the mirror, is shocked. She doesn't turn around.

Huma Nina?
Nina . . .

With incandescent resolve, Nina holds out a wrist and cuts it with a razor blade: blood.

Nina!

EIGHT

*Spotlight on the microphone. Nothing happens. Then
Agrado, in her Chanel, steps into the light, taps the
microphone, peers out nervously.*

Agrado One, two, two. Two.

Ladies and gentlemen, could I have your attention
please? Good evening. I'm very sorry . . . but something's
gone wrong. I could say it's a technical hitch, but that
would be a lie: it's human, like most hitches. Suffice to say
that owing to circumstances beyond the management's
control, we have to cancel. House lights, please.

Nothing happens.

Pablo?

Pablo, black me out.

The spotlight remains.

Please.

(*Is very upset. Tries again.*) Ladies and gentlemen . . .
Huma Rojo and Nina Cruz . . . my friends . . . who
perform so brilliantly on this stage every night, can't be
here . . . *A Streetcar Named Desire* has been cancelled . . .

There's an usher. See if you can prise a . . .

Pablo . . . please . . .

I don't want it . . .

Stop. Stop. Stop.

*Deadly silence. A breakdown, as if the actor playing
Agrado in* All About My Mother *has had enough. And
then Esteban steps into the spotlight, with his own
microphone. Agrado stares, amazed.*

Esteban Five seconds of dead stage time feels like an
hour, you know: speak.

(*Mimics her gently.*) Your name's Agrado, and you're
very authentic and your eyes are shaped like diamonds.

A moment.

Agrado You think so?

Esteban Perfect diamonds.

Agrado That was the intention.
Cher was the inspiration.

Esteban How much?

Agrado Eighty thousand pesetas. Bargain.

Esteban Is that a Chanel?

Agrado Nothing like it to make you feel respectable.

Esteban Is it real?

Agrado You really want to know?

Esteban They do.

Agrado Of course not.

Esteban How much was your nose?

Agrado I know you're not interested . . .

Esteban One-seven-five?

Agrado Two hundred. Cash down the pan as a year later
some scumbag decided to work on it with his fists – now
it's bent to buggery. Mind you, it adds to my personality,
don't you think –?

She turns to Esteban, but he isn't there. It throws her.
She peers out to the audience. She resumes, tentatively.

Still . . . if I'd known it was going to be mashed I wouldn't
have bothered having it done.
    My tits, however, were worth every penny: paid for
themselves ten times over . . .

[**Mario from Theatre Box** How much was the silicone?

98

Agrado Premature interjection, honey, I was getting to that . . .] [Silicone is] a hundred thousand a litre, and I have it everywhere, lips, brows, cheeks, hips and bum, so you do the sums, I lost count years ago. (*And now she has hit her stride again.*) Jaw reduction, seventy-five. Impressive, Pablo, I know. And that's it really, ladies and gentlemen. Me. Every part made to measure. You see, wasn't that better than going back out to drag-queen hell? The lesson? It costs a packet to be authentic. But you can't be stingy when it comes to your appearance.

Una es más auténtica cuando más se parece a lo que ha soñado de sí misma: you are more authentic, the more you resemble the dream you have of yourself.

At this point there are two ways to end this scene.

Agrado could say:

Agrado And I'm done.

She curtsies, and the spotlight fades slowly. End of scene.

Alternatively, she could say:

Agrado And I'm done. (*Curtsies.*)
House lights, Pablo.

House lights up.

Oh, hello! Remember me? It's Señor and Señora Rock Hudson, ladies and gentlemen: let's not go back over old ground.

She walks offstage and circles the stalls, ad libbing to audience members along these lines.

I thank you . . . Yes, señor, very authentic . . . No, no touching . . . I'm retired, but see me at the end in the bar and I'll sing you a filthy song . . . (*Waves to upper circle.*) Thanks to you too, cheap people! . . . Many thanks . . . So glad you stayed . . . Oooh, Germans, they've nabbed the best seats . . . Heavens, you're not still alive? . . . English? Yes, I can smell the yeast. Ninety-four per cent of my clients were alcoholics, ninety-three per cent came from Sedgefield . . . Oh, the devastated football fan! I remember you! In 1994, Barcelona thumped Manchester United four–nil, and he was inconsolable, there was nothing I could do, I sucked like a Hoover, but he just cried . . . For you, darling, I'd come out of retirement if you want me to finish you off. Thank you . . . thank you . . . many thanks, my friends . . .

An Usher opens a door for her to leave the stalls.

And aren't the ushers here delectable? I do approve. Good night.

The house lights snap out as she leaves the stalls. End of scene.

NINE

Sister Rosa, in a hospital bed. She is heavily pregnant. There are things serene, determined and forgiving about her.

Sister Rosa I want some water.

Manuela You can't . . .

Sister Rosa One sip.

Manuela relents, helps her sip from a bottle of water.

Manuela I think your mother wants me to go.

Sister Rosa She doesn't. She understands, I know it. (*Looks at view.*) What a day.

Manuela. I want you to promise me something. If anything happens . . .

Manuela What's going to happen?

Sister Rosa I can hardly pick up a pencil . . .

Manuela Rosa –

Sister Rosa No, it's all right . . .

Manuela You'll be OK.

Sister Rosa Manuela . . .

Manuela You'll get stronger.

Sister Rosa Promise me you'll never keep any secrets from him.

Manuela I don't have to, Rosa, you can tell him / yourself –

Sister Rosa Promise, promise.

Manuela All right. If it makes you happy.

Sister Rosa This child has to know everything. Promise.

Manuela I promise.

Enter Mother.

Mother You'll be in theatre within the hour.

Sister Rosa Thank you, Mama.

Manuela is on one side of Sister Rosa's bed, Mother the other.

Look at the Barceloneta. Beautiful.

Mother Do you think?

Sister Rosa Yes!

Mother It was very different when you were little. We never came anywhere near it, but I preferred it back then.

Sister Rosa I'd like to be down there, swimming.

Mother Soon.

Sister Rosa takes Mother's hand. They are intimate as never before.

Sister Rosa How's your work?

Mother Mine?

Sister Rosa Yes, aren't I allowed to be interested?

Mother Oh . . . well . . . I'm sending the latest Chagall to a buyer in London.

Sister Rosa Good.

Mother Pity he doesn't want my Picassos. I'd make a fortune. Not to be: the easiest to copy and the hardest to sell.
One day I hope you'll be able to sell them.
You're not in any pain?

Sister Rosa Not a bit.

Mother Pregnancy without the pain. You should write the manual.

Sister Rosa You don't have to stay, Mama, if you don't want to.

Mother Do you want me to go?

Sister Rosa No. But if you want to . . .

Mother Don't be silly, of course I don't want to. You're mine.

A moment.

Sister Rosa I didn't kiss Papa goodbye. Will you give him one from me?

Mother I'm keeping this one for myself.

She kisses her. Sister Rosa smiles.

Sister Rosa Mama.

Mother Yes.

Sister Rosa Mama.

Mother My child . . .

The actor playing Sister Rosa removes herself from All About My Mother. *Bleep.*

My child.

Bleep.

My child.

Bleeeep.
Manuela and Mother are alone on either side of the empty bed. The sounds of the hospital. Then silence.

TEN

Spotlight on Esteban, with the microphone.

Esteban I see myself one day with a microphone in a lecture hall, talking about what it took to write my stories, just like Truman Capote in his preface to *Music for Chameleons*. I'll be the figure from the dust-jacket photo, spilling his guts about the moment when he learnt the brutal difference between good and great art; the writer, freed from his desk for one night only to initiate an audience into the mysteries of creation.

Soon after the beginning of this speech, the convention is broken as the spotlight begins to bleed: harsh afternoon light floods the scene, revealing Manuela, on a bench in a dusty city square with palm trees and a fountain, cradling a baby, humming; and Agrado watching from the distance; and, walking towards Manuela from Agrado, a striking, disturbing female figure. Esteban, speaking at the microphone, is at first unaware that he is not alone.

I'm seventeen today, the exact age Capote was when he decided he was ready to publish after a childhood perfecting his craft. There's this competition in Alicante, and once I've finished this new story, I'm going to enter –

The microphone cracks or whines. He taps it.

– the first steps towards my own preface and sharing everything I'm writing here at this precise moment with strangers whose lives have been profoundly changed by words I . . .

By which point the light is fiercely bright, the microphone has stopped working, and Esteban is aware that he is no longer on his own. He turns. The figure has reached Manuela. Esteban drops the arm holding the microphone to his side, stares.

Lola Manuela . . .

Manuela Don't say anything.

Lola How is he . . . ?

Manuela I said don't.
   I looked for you. I should have known I'd have to wait till someone died before we met.
   Rosa needed you, Lola.

Lola I had to go home to Argentina. I had to see it again.
   You haven't changed . . .

Manuela What is it? What makes you want to take the most beautiful thing in the world and just . . .

Lola I went to our house.

Manuela Stop.

Lola I had to say goodbye.
  I'm tired, Manuela. I'm dying.

Manuela No, you *are* death. (*Stands, a change of heart.*)
I shouldn't have agreed to this – go back to Agrado.

Lola I won't give up till I've seen him.

Manuela (*calls*) Agrado! You're too late.

Lola Let me.

Manuela You're too / late –

Lola Please.

Manuela (*turns on her*) You're not a human being, Lola,
you're an epidemic!

  Agrado approaches; the baby and Manuela are crying.

Shhh . . . shhhh . . .

Agrado Manolita . . .

Manuela It's all right . . .

Lola I'm his father.

Manuela It's all right . . .

  *She is saying all this to Agrado as well as to the baby.
  Agrado tries to move Lola away.*

Agrado This isn't the time . . .

Lola Manuela . . .

Manuela You have no right!

  She pulls herself together. A moment.

He isn't your only son.

Lola What . . . ?

Manuela When I left Barcelona, I was pregnant with your child.
 A boy.

Lola You had him . . . ?

Manuela He was beautiful, precious.

Lola Where is he?

Manuela You can't see him.

Lola Manuela . . .

Manuela I won't let you . . .
 He died, eight months ago . . . a car . . .
 That's why I came back, Lola.

She takes Esteban's notebook from her handbag, gives it to her.

Look at the last entry.

She retreats into the distance with the baby. Agrado looks to Lola, then follows Manuela. Lola is on her own: she has to sit. She opens the notebook as if it were alive.

Esteban I found this old photo of my mother last night. She's standing in front of a shack on some beach, and she's wearing this massive straw hat, and she's smiling like she's tripping. It's like a portal into a time I wasn't alive – but I'm not allowed through, because the photo's been ripped in half.

He sits on the bench next to her.

I'm starting to think that this is something like half a life. Then I get scared I'll always feel this way, which makes the idea of growing older seem pointless. So what the fuck is that, a suicidal tendency? None of the stuff I pretend matters matters, not the story about the actresses, nor the competition; I'd throw it all in if I could put the photo back together, because then I could look into his eyes and I'd know if he'd have been proud of me. I'm so disappointed with Mama. I saw her in that transplant simulation, she was acting the truth for strangers, yet she pretends to *me*. I don't want to be angry with her, but I am. I've a right to know all about my father. She can't deny me my right.

Lola cries. Manuela returns with the baby. Agrado has gone.

Lola Manuela –

Manuela Shhh. You have to let me do this my way, or I'm leaving.

A moment. She sits next to Lola, then holds the baby. Lola takes him carefully.

He's the spitting image of Rosa . . .

We go to the doctor every week . . . he's been so often I think he looks forward to it.

Agrado says you went to the nuns.

Lola (*nods*) They told me about Rosa . . .

Manuela Do you think they knew she was HIV positive?

Lola No.

Manuela You have to promise me you won't go anywhere near her mother.

Lola I never met her.

Manuela Keep it that way.

She doesn't know you . . . and you've devastated her . . . She's paranoid about infection . . .

Sometimes I feel like kidnapping him and taking him to Madrid.

We're just going to have to keep working at her, aren't we, Esteban? Grandma Rosa's going to have to get used to us, hmm?

Lola Can I kiss him?

Manuela For goodness' sake, of course you can.

Lola Esteban . . . I'm sorry for the awful inheritance I'm leaving you.

Manuela Stop that . . . you don't understand, Lola. He's well. The only thing that matters is now: and today he's healthy. Mother-to-child transmission isn't a given . . . her Caesarean helped . . . he's healthy . . . and do you know, I think Grandma knows that. The problem isn't him, it's that she never knew her own daughter.
(*Picks up notebook.*) He wrote in this every day . . . he never let it out of his sight.
(*Takes photograph out of her handbag.*) Esteban.

Lola You called him Esteban?

Manuela (*nods*) I just never got around to telling him why.
Keep it. (*Re. notebook.*) This is mine.

Lola hands back the baby; Manuela gives him the photograph.

Lola Thank you.

Manuela hums to the baby. Lola watches.

Manuela What was it between you and Rosa, Lola?

Lola I'd never met anyone like her. People were just people to her.

Manuela I wish I could say that was a good thing.

Lola I never knew where to draw the line, did I?

Manuela Too much of everything. That's what Agrado says about you.
Look, Esteban. It's Papa. Papa the Pioneer.

Esteban turns to her. For the first time since Madrid, Manuela looks into his face.

Papa.

Lola, meanwhile, looks to the baby and softly sings a half-forgotten tune:

Lola
It's a Barnum and Bailey world . . .

La-las lines.

                              . . . make-believe
If you believed . . . in me.

Esteban walks off, disappearing forever. Manuela watches him go. Manuela, Lola and the baby Esteban.

ELEVEN

Agrado, in black, on the floor with the baby Esteban in a bouncy-chair/rocker, at Sister Rosa's Mother's.

Agrado Stop growing. Stop it . . . too fast . . .!
How do I look? Personally, I can't stand Death's fetish for black. Some kitsch wouldn't have gone astray – your papa loved kitsch, especially at funerals, it was a great quality of hers. One of many. Because whatever they say, Esteban, Lola wasn't all bad. True, no amount of surgical work was ever going to hide her vast thighs, but she did have some good points. She was life itself when I first met her. My compadre in tits! (*Becomes tearful.*) I just want you to know that when he came back it was because of you . . . He turned up on my doorstep looking like something the cat spat out . . . I was so angry, he'd stolen my rings, wigs, all my silver toilet articles . . . but he came back because of you.

Enter Huma during the following, in black, with a plate of food.

So when they go dancing on his grave, you come and see your Auntie Agrado. Your rich grandmother's a very nice lady but she wouldn't know a good time if it sat on her face, so you know my number in times of family tension.

We can take mutually beneficial field trips to the park. And I have an idea for matching tattoos. And when you're old enough, if you want them, I'll pay for your tits.

Perhaps Huma clears her throat.

Oops . . . Doña Huma the spinster.

Huma Corrupting the child?

Agrado That's what aunts are for.

Huma Be careful what you say about Lola in front of Rosa's mother.

Agrado Today was hard for me as well . . .

Huma I know, Agradito . . .

Agrado I loved her. Yes, she was a monster, but she was my monster. (*Tears.*) All I'm saying, Esteban, is that the send-off for a bitch like your papa should have been a bit drug-fucked. It's what she would have wanted.

Huma Shhh . . .

Enter Manuela and Isabel, both in black, with more food.

Manuela How is he?

Huma Adorable. More and more like his mama.

A chorus of oohing and aahing and chatter as they put the food down and gather round the rocker.

Isabel Hello, lovely little man!

Manuela He's got her eyes, hasn't he . . . ?

Huma She'd be so proud.

Agrado But he's growing up too quickly!

Huma Is Grandmother joining us?

Manuela She needs a moment . . .

Huma It wasn't easy for her today . . .

Agrado I can't believe she asked us back!

Manuela Honestly, I think all she wanted was to make sure he was really gone.

Huma Agrado, don't cry . . .

Agrado I'm sorry, Manuela, it's just that Lola and I would spend long hours in cheap Paris restaurants planning the most extravagant funerals, and that one was a bit monochrome.

Manuela I agree. (*Kisses her.*)

Agrado Oh, do something, Esteban: please turn Papa's funeral into a fiesta.

They look at the baby; he does something; peals of laughter.

Agrado Oh, Manolita, Manolita! Look at you!

Huma You're a family.

Mother Yes.

She has appeared in a doorway. They turn to look at her.

Why is nobody eating . . . ?

Manuela Come in, Rosa.

Mother We wouldn't have invited you if we didn't want you to eat.

They do, in silence. Agrado cries.

Agrado I'm sorry, señora. I have two real things in my life: silicone and feelings.

Mother Empanadas?

Agrado I couldn't. (*Taps her figure.*)

Isabel Is he hungry?

Mother He's just fussing.

Huma Will you ever go back to work, Manuela?

Manuela One day.

Mother I hope not. Now I've got two new people to spend my money on . . .
  She can though, of course, if that's what she wants.

Manuela When Esteban's older. Though as a nurse, not an actress.

Isabel Oh, don't say that! Everyone in the *Streetcar* company thought you were miles better than Nina –

She stops herself. A moment.

Mother Is something the matter?

Huma No.
  Nina's been knocked up by some hick from her village, that's all.

A moment. Agrado contains a giggle.

Agrado (*to Mother, confidentially*) Her junkie ex-lover.

Mother Oh.

Agrado (*to Manuela, confidentially*) The latest is they're getting married.

Manuela Perhaps it's for the best.

Huma Obviously I don't think so . . . I think she's thrown her life away.

Agrado The man is fat.

Mother Would anyone like wine?

Manuela Good idea.

Agrado Very fat. Ugly, inbred, spotty, very ugly . . . fat.

Manuela sings to baby Esteban. Isabel joins in. Mother pours the wine.

Isabel Is he well?

Manuela Pardon?

Isabel Will he always be . . . well?

A moment. Mother is doing her very best.

Mother It's all right.
There's no reason he should should become ill.
Would you like a drink, Huma?

Huma Thank you, Rosa.

Mother Good health.

Huma Good health.

Mother And . . . how's your play?

Huma Ongoing.

Mother What is it?

Huma We don't need to talk about it . . .

Mother But I'd like to know.

Huma *Blood Wedding.*

Mother Lorca?

Huma nods.

Agrado She's stupendous, a hit, the man obviously foresaw Huma in a dream and wrote it for her. And you too, Isabel, you're quite good.

Isabel You'll all have to come and see it – we leave for Madrid at the end of the month.

Manuela I don't see Esteban giving me a night off. Your earring's loose, Huma.

Huma (*to Agrado*) Sort it out, you animal.

Agrado (*barks*) There isn't an animal alive who'd / do what I –

Their chatter has recommenced, but they are interrupted.

Mother I'd like to hear a speech from it, Huma.
    I didn't know ... Lola ... I hate what I've heard.
    I don't know how you can cry for him. He took my daughter. He murdered Rosa.
    But you're right, that was a terrible, friendless funeral ... Not even he ...
    He must have had a mother.
    That's all.

Huma We should go.

Mother No, I want you to stay.

Huma Rosa ... I don't think *Blood Wedding* would really be appropriate / for –

Mother You are mistaken, señora, it would be completely appropriate, and every single one of you knows it.

She has shocked them with her vehemence.

Huma Manuela ...

Mother Never mind, Lorca's obviously only for actors, I'm sorry I asked: eat, eat, eat, all of / you eat –

Isabel We need lots of grandsons!

It's a nervously delivered cue. They all look to her. Manuela looks to Huma.

   Isabel We need lots of grandsons.

A moment.

Manuela Rosa wants it, Huma . . . and we're in her house. It's all right. I know it; I know what's coming. Something about it taking a long time.

A moment.

> **Huma** We need granddaughters, too.
>
> **Isabel** I'd like it to happen in a day. For our children to have two or three strapping men just like that.
>
> **Huma** That's not the way of it. It takes a long time. That's why it's unbearable to see your child's blood spilled on the ground. A spring that streams for a moment though we've paid with years. When I got to my son, he was lying in the middle of the street. I bathed my hands in his blood and licked it with my tongue. Because it was mine. Because animals lick their young. You don't know what that means. If I could, I would put that earth, blushed with his blood, into a holy cup.
>
> Be quiet. My son should answer. But my son is already an armful of dried flowers. My son is already a dark voice beyond the mountains. Be quiet. No weeping here. Your tears come from your eyes only; when mine come I'll be alone, and they'll come from the soles of my feet, from my very roots, and they'll burn hotter than blood.

Five women in black, marooned within All About My Mother *actors, crew and theatre.*

End.